Believe *you* can!

- Become the person you would truly like to be
- Overcome the effects of redundancy or economic defeat
- Acquire the habit of success and self-confidence

Allen Carmichael

By the same author:
'MULTI-LEVEL MARKETING'
ISBN 1 873288 00 X
Concept July 1990
2nd Edition – retitled 'NETWORK AND MULTI-LEVEL MARKETING'
ISBN 1 873288 01 8
Concept September 1991

'THE NETWORK MARKETING SELF-STARTER
ISBN 1 873288 02 6
Concept November 1991

ISBN 1 873288 03 4

Design and production by Dinah Parkinson
Cover design by Allen Carmichael
Typeset by Cambrian Typesetters, Frimley, Surrey
Printed in Great Britain by Cox & Wyman, Reading

CONTENTS

	Introduction	1
1.	The start	9
2.	The challenge	11
3.	The nature of motivation	21
4.	All in the mind	27
5.	The beginnings of change	39
6.	Taking control	45
7.	Turning things around	55
8.	Recognition and reward	61
9.	False limitations	69
10.	Winner and losers	75
11.	The importance of success	81
12.	The look of success	85
13.	Motivation through expectation	91
14.	Learning and the need for programming	97
15.	Conditioning for success	103
16.	Putting it all together	115
17.	Acquiring the habit of success	127
18.	The final move!	139
19.	The end of the journey – or just the beginning	145
20.	P.S.	149

For S. M. P.

– there could have been no greater, more sympathetic, encouraging, or more understanding support.

'Sometimes a book . . . taken up at random,
merely with the object of reading it as a pastime,
has been known to call forth energies whose existence
had not before been suspected.'

Samuel Smiles 1859

INTRODUCTION

This book is very much the product of my own experience and observation. Whilst I certainly cannot claim any professional or medical qualification as a justification for its production, I can claim what I see as my greatest attribute – *simply being a human being*, experiencing what others experience and being able to observe what is observable by all of us.

None of us is perfect and most of us, if we are to be perfectly honest, would willingly admit that life has not brought us everything we feel it might have. So the possibility and potential for change and improvement is something available to all of us – and something from which almost everyone could benefit. If, as they say, you are not part of the solution, you must be part of the problem!

What is success? It is really, I suppose, the accomplishment of aims, and, as such, a very personal thing, relative to our own circumstances and aspirations, and bearing little relationship to that which we perceive to be the success of others. It is all things to all men. It is important to decide just what it means to you. Is it, for example, the attainment of great wealth? Is it the achievement of long-standing ambitions? Is it to become a better person?

It might be all of these things – or none of them. Success is a purely personal thing, a sensation, a tangible entity or a continuing experience which grows and develops, fed by the adrenalin that it itself produces. Is it something that others can see, sense or benefit from by association?

It is all these things – and more.

We are all surprisingly vulnerable, and this, I think, is the fundamental charm of human beings. It doesn't matter how high anyone may climb, or with what visible signs and tokens of success they may surround themselves, beneath the surface people are all – in the broadest possible sense – very much the same, very much alone and accountable for themselves and their actions – and each and every one is vulnerable to the same strokes of fate or fortune. To some these may represent disaster, to others triumph but, in the main, they are transient happenings as nobody can remain on a peak for ever – or indeed wallow in a trough indefinitely! Human beings are extraordinarily resilient and have a vast capacity for both revival and survival.

At the end of March 1992 Dunn & Bradstreet reported that 160 small businesses were collapsing every day. This is an alarming fact, but what was not reported with the same degree of interest by the media was the number of new businesses starting up over the same period. The fact that hundreds may have failed in one particular field will never deter another person from believing they can succeed at the same thing. Thank goodness things are this way! Recession cannot continue for ever, nor is it something that can be switched off like a light. It is more like a super tanker moving along with a momentum that needs the distance of 7 miles to stop. Recovery will be slow, but things *will* change, fortunes *will* be made, and good will come out of adversity.

This book then, is dedicated to the concept of change – change that is possible for anyone. Change that should result in you becoming the person you would like to be and in achieving the things you truly desire.

Having said that, I have always contended that people *do not change* – that the leopard is stuck with his spots. However people can be modified, and through that modification, the circumstances that surround them will change to some degree as well. This is simply because of the influences they bring to bear on those circumstances.

It is a fact that opportunity and new beginnings have frequently been the direct result of adversity. It is all too easy, through complacency, to allow oneself to slide, almost unnoticed, into a life of comforting and boring routine. It has been said that the difference between a rut and a grave is only a matter of depth. In routine lies what might appear to be security but modern life has shown all too many people the folly of that particular assumption.

We live in times where the unexpected is constantly happening – and has indeed almost become the expected. Job-loss, redundancy and business collapse are no longer exceptional circumstances. But, that in no way alters or invalidates the devastating effects these sombre events can have on the individuals who have experienced them first-hand. To have one's life disturbed and disrupted by the suddeness of such happenings could never be described as pleasant or desirable but, in a curious way, these events could actually acquire value by being the means of opening tired eyes to the realities of life – and particularly to new opportunity and a realization of latent potential.

So, to attempt to bring about change – or, if you prefer it, modification – we need to have an understanding of some of the factors that have made us the people we are. Each one of us is the sum of everything that has happened to us in life so far. We have been moulded and shaped by influences over which we had little control as well as by influences we, of our own free will, created. If modification is possible, we need to know what to modify! Human beings are very adaptable providing they are in control of a situation. Control, however, may have been allowed to slip away so that circumstances are dictating events rather than the individual being in control of his or her own situation.

All actions and circumstances are the result of mental attitudes and by understanding something of the mechanics of your mind in simple terms, you are acquiring a tool of considerable value.

I have always believed that patterns will inevitably repeat themselves. In an interview situation with, say, a job applicant, I would always look for the emergence of any kind of pattern since that can be taken as a pointer towards future actions and attitudes. This, however, is only true up to a point: patterns can be altered and disturbed if there is a real DESIRE for change, and BELIEF in that possibility.

So, given that one requirement – desire for change – it is possible to modify ourselves and re-evaluate circumstances and attitudes to produce a plan for survival, and to use the building bricks of that plan to aid us in seeking, recognizing and exploiting new opportunities.

We may see our situation as being full of problems. Anything that can be said to have a solution is not really a problem. However, difficulties are different: they have to be faced, worked through and dispelled.

We live in a world in which there appears to be a reluctance to use honest straight-forward words to express basic concepts. Redundancy doesn't become any easier to accept because it is referred to as 'de-hiring', 'accelerated retirement', 'contractural dis-engagement', 'stimulated second opportunity' or simply 'out-placement'. Anyone who has experienced redundancy knows just how frightening it can be to have the sudden realization that one no longer has a job and that, as of that moment, the pay cheques have ceased and will no longer appear with the comforting regularity that has been the norm.

There is a sober finality about clearing out one's desk or work place, eyes surreptitiously watching in the awed silence as one bears away the residual flotsam of a career in a supermarket carrier bag. The cheery promises, made from behind the barricade of temporary security, of maintaining contact, have a hollow ring about them.

It is recognized by psychiatrists that the stress caused by redundancy is on a par with the suffering experienced after the death of a close relative or friend. There is actually a kind of grieving process that many people go through, and it can easily take up to a year to recover. Even when redundancy is a distinct possibility and is expected, like death under similar circumstances, it is still a devastating blow when it comes.

It is the blow to self-esteem that is the hardest to bear. To be singled out perhaps from a group of equally competent workers and marked for redundancy – although it may have nothing whatsoever to do with job performance – seems tantamount to a suggestion of incompetence or the inability to do the job properly.

Ends and beginnings . . .

In a world where human relationships are based very much on the 'child/parent' roles, redundancy will often cause the individual to move their stance from the role of 'parent' to that of 'child' with all the resultant reactions that implies. It is vital to reinstate the parent role with the minimum of delay. Feelings of worthlessness must not be allowed to develop into that devastating downward spiral – a situation so difficult to reverse. How well one survives such an experience depends on exactly how the circumstances are tackled.

Consider the following points:

* The greatest possible support can come from a

truly sympathetic spouse or partner. A display of sympathy is not what is required for this can so often fuel the feelings of anger and self-pity. An attitude of optimism and expectation coupled with a determination to turn things around will act as the greatest stimulants.

* It is vitally important to act immediately so as not to allow feelings of self-pity to develop and lull one into a state of tired and resentful inactivity. The classic situation here is to go to bed early, get up late, sit slumped before a television set and show every sign of withdrawal from normal human contact.

* It is essential to get rid of all the natural feelings of resentment, frustration, and the seeming insult at being cast aside in such a cavalier fashion.

* It is essential to forget feelings of the 'after-all-I-did-for-them' sort and face up to the concept of a new challenge which must be acted upon with the minimum of delay.

This may be the greatest opportunity life has yet proffered. That might be difficult to appreciate at this stage, perhaps – the disguise is so complete. Change is always the greatest tonic – something akin to being pushed over a precipice and finding that you have survived!

In my own particular voyage of discovery, activated by circumstances certainly not of my choosing, I unearthed a whole new career and, through that bumpy journey learned a great deal that I consider worth passing on to you, my reader. I cannot claim to have found the complete answer as survival is still, to some extent, the name of the game. But all the indications are that the light at the end of the tunnel may not, after all, be an on-coming train!

The answers for each and every one of us will be entirely different. Obviously anything I write cannot turn you into someone else – but I think I can offer you hope and change. I ask only one thing of you – don't approach this book with too much questioning scepticism – give it a go – *believe* in yourself and the fact that it is possible to set a chain of events in motion that you have not perhaps totally planned. I am confident that I can offer you a route, a lifeboat – or whatever it is you need or you care to call it – that will enable you to see and understand the real possiblity of becoming the person you would truly like to be.

Allen Carmichael
September 1992

THE START

At the commencement of any book the decision the author is faced with is exactly where to begin. Self-improvement, change and development need one simple ingredient to act as the blue touch-paper which will ignite them – desire. Desire is the motivation, the driving force of life. This is, of course, an immensely broad subject; a book of this nature will be read by people in all walks of life and in a diversity of occupations, each one of them looking at the purchase they have made with varying degrees of expectation.

Subjectively, 'motivation' is very often linked to sales success and is the purpose of endless seminars and rah-rah conventions, whipping a flagging sales force into a new frenzy of activity. Enormous sums of money are expended every year on these exercises, – all tax-deductible of course – in attempting to show people how to fulfil their own potential within the organization that is footing the bill.

But motivation concerns us all and affects every aspect of our daily lives. We all suffer emotional ups and downs, all the tragedies, triumphs and disappointments life can fling at us. We all go through periods of indecision when we feel we are lacking any sense of direction. These are the occasions when a greater understanding of how we tick, and, more importantly, how we could be made to tick more effectively, can be of immense value.

And so, I have not tried to relate this book to any specific circumstances or professional fields, but, rather to keep the subject as open and fluid as possible. This, I hope, will satisfy most people since to please all of the people all of the time is, most likely, a vain expectation!

Some years ago an American architect was commissioned to design a new department store on the West Coast of the United States. He began by visiting the proposed site and climbing to the highest point where he sat down to admire the wonderful view his vantage point offered whilst he awaited inspiration. It was obvious to him that where he was sitting had to be the centre of the restaurant so he took out his sketch pad and designed the cover for the book of matches that would eventually go on the tables! The whole concept for the building developed outwards from that simple beginning to become a unified and cohesive whole.

So, a starting point we must have. Every journey, no matter how long or complex, starts with just one step . . . and that step is commitment.

Positive action:
1. Decide right now that you are committed to bettering your circumstances in any way you can. Prepare yourself to do something to create change and bring added value to the quality of your life.
2. Write down your feelings as a declaration of intent. And write down WHY you have decided on this course of action.

2. THE CHALLENGE

Take heart – don't be afraid! Look about you and seek opportunity . . .

Where have you come from?
Where are you now?
Where are you going?
What have you done to make sure you will get there?

When, I wonder, did you last review you circumstances and evaluate your situation by answering those four vital questions?

Try doing it right now – being totally honest with yourself. This is the starting point of our voyage of self-discovery and revelation. Take a blank sheet of paper and write down your answers in as much detail as you can before you read any further. Don't cheat on yourself – leave turning the page until you have completed this task to your complete satisfaction.

Looking at your answers you may realize that where you have come from is not perhaps as relevant to the purposes of this exercise as where you are now – which, of course, is the direct result of choices you have already made, probably in the distant past. But are you satisfied with the outcome of those decisions? Did you make the right choices? Was it a difficult route you travelled or were all the options easy? Do you feel satisfied and fulfilled by the way things have worked out? Is life still offering challenge or has the excitement been replaced by apparently unalterable routine? Or, are you the victim of circumstances over which you feel you have had little or no control, with a future that seems to offer very little indeed.

Every day is full of choices, and if your present situation or state is the result of choices you made in the past, it has got to be that the choices you are free to make NOW will affect your future. In the financial services industry there used to be a favourite question asked of a client – 'how much did you earn over the past ten years?' When the client had worked out the answer, the next question was – 'and how much of that sum do you have now?' The client was always surprised to realize what a lot of money had slipped through his or her fingers without very much to show for it. The point the salesman was making was to suggest that something could be done *now* to make sure that at the end of the next ten years, the situation would be somewhat different.

Precisely similar thoughts can apply to life in general. How well did we utilize the past ten years?

Doesn't it seem vitally important to spend some time over the consideration of choices and decisions you could make now to be sure they will be the right ones for your future?

You may be one of the casualties of this new decade, a victim of recession, suffering redundancy or the loss of not only a job, but possibly even your own business. On the other hand, you might have reached that point in life at which you have fulfilled all the potential a far-sighted employer recognized in you – you may even have suffered the fate of so many people – a curious phenomenon that is characteristic of many large oganizations – of having been promoted to your level of incompetence! This, of course, is the end of the line so far as any further promotion is possible. The only moves from this dubious position are sideways.

This point is often reached in the pattern of an individual's career, between the ages of say 40 and 50. There are still 15 to 25 working years ahead. What a prospect! – especially if one is aware that further advancement is unlikely. There are far too many people who bemoan the fact that they really would have liked to have done something different with their lives. Unfortunately when one points out that it is never too late to start a new career, two particular thoughts bubble to the surface. The complacent situation about which they are mildly complaining has very often eroded away energy levels to such an extent that the worry arises as to whether they could actually achieve anything new. The second thought is much more practical – the worry that pension rights and other perks with which their job is probably surrounded might be jeopardized.

Let boldness be your friend! You must weigh the short term inconveniences against the long term benefits. Allow yourself the luxury of speculation. Surely this is the point in life at which any sensible person should do a serious stock-take. It is the perfect time for change and for new beginnings, new directions. There is the opportunity to cast off the occupation that has become threadbare through association and seek new challenges that could put the sparkle back into life. That sparkle comes with change.

As I have already pointed out though, far too many people are walled around with pension schemes, death-in-service benefits and profit-sharing schemes and a variety of other nails that have been systematically hammered through their coat tails by an employer determined to ensure continued loyalty and service. It takes a bold person to launch themselves into a programme of change, resulting, perhaps, in a completely new career. We only get one stab at this life so surely there is every argument in favour of making the best of it in every way?

Of course it is not everyone that can bring themselves to think in this way. If it comes to making a dramatic decision that could completely alter the course of one's life for the better, you would think the choice should be easy. But there are many people who simply could not face up to that as a proposition. One can feel sympathy for those who find themselves trapped by the seduction of continued employment – even in a job for which they no longer have any real feeling – as their only means of maintaining the financial burdens with which they have surrounded themselves.

Redundancy and job-loss therefore, though no sane person would seek either state willingly, can be the shock treatment that might set a whole train of events in motion.

So, where are you going? Have you made any choices or decisions? If you haven't, the likelihood is that your life will drift on in an unexciting way until you reach its inevitable conclusion.

'Where are you going', of course, can only be related to decisions of a purely temporary nature – unless you have a rigid plan and intend to stick to it, allowing no possibility of deflection or deviation. Georges Braque, the French painter, when talking about creativity used to say that if it was possible to visualize a finished picture in your mind with such clarity and vividness that all you had to do was to put it on canvas, the result would be worthless. He contended that the hand of creativity would not have touched such a work. Rather, the painter should approach everything with a totally open mind since it is the exploitation of the accidental that is the true basis of all creativity. He may set out with a vivid mental picture of his aim but, inevitably, things will happen on the journey towards that goal which will alter his intention and, at this exciting moment when creativity takes over, produce results far beyond the original visualization. This then is the nature of creativity.

As we travel through life we are constantly faced with forks in the road, a choice of two possible directions where important decisions must be made. I believe that providing one always goes for the more difficult option there should never be cause for regret. The easy option, though temporarily fulfilling, rarely leads to permanent satisfaction.

So, did you take the scenic route of easy options on your journey to where you find yourself today? – or did you travel the more difficult rugged and challenging route? If you could do it all again, would you make any changes?

Have you thought about the possibility of change? Have you considered that you could be the master of your own destiny and, if you haven't actually achieved a great deal in life so far, there is still unlimited opportunity for success to be yours? The possibility is always available and lies very much in your own hands, requiring from you only one thing to set change in motion – *desire*. Nobody can push you as far as you are able to push yourself.

Success is never going to spring out of the woodwork and take you by surprise – it must be planned and anticipated.

Does your present job, assuming you have one, have the potential to alter your future? What, indeed, would you ask of that future? If you could start again, what would you change?

* If you had the choice, where would you really like to live?
* Do you have aspirations?
* What car would you like to drive?
* How do you visualize your ideal lifestyle?

Everyone has dreams . . . but, so far, how near has the reality of your life come to those dreams?

This book is not intended to be a textbook or training manual. The intention is to encourage *you* to do the work, to explore yourself, ask questions of yourself – and even question the answers. The book will not answer all the questions for you. What it should do is to make you think. The experiences into which you may well be lead – always providing you remain open and receptive to them – will help to clarify your future moves and, hopefully, the route you should follow. Any attempt at a process of change can result in odd, strange and even bizarre experiences but these are part of the learning curve of change and modification. Be prepared for the unexpected and be ready to respond to the ideas and hunches that may come to you. Aim always to be alert and responsive for life will surely confront you with surprises and rewards for your efforts.

It doesn't matter how old you are, it is never too late to make changes, to strive towards new goals, and, hopefully, to end up by asking yourself why you didn't do something like this years ago? The fact is, you didn't – and looking over your shoulder never achieved anything – so let's get down to this business of change, and do something about it now!

My hope is that this book may prove to be your guide to changes that could effect the whole of your future by enabling you to journey towards the realization of whatever your particular and personal dream may be. Don't wait for things to happen – make them happen!

We like to think that some people are luckier than others. Look at the people you consider as lucky. I am sure you will find that they are amongst the most lively and industrious people you know. We can create our own luck by going out and making things happen.

On meeting a writer or painter, in fact anyone creative, most people assume theirs is a wonderful life in which work is only necessary when inspiration strikes. If this was the case not a lot would happen, and very few would survive! Inspiration often has to be forced from its hiding place by sheer hard work – in other words by creating the right circumstances – the fertile ground in which the frail plant can grow and flourish. Forcing the pace by pushing hard, even though nothing of worth seems to be happening at that moment. Then quite suddenly, out of this strife and effort, the spark appears that ignites the real fire. There is nothing magical about this; it is simply the workings of what I call the Human Dynamo, of which you will hear a lot more as you read on.

Never, never lose sight of this – success is a journey, not a destination . . .

Positive action:

1. Fully answer the questions on page 11. Did you do this?
2. Consider in detail the questions on page 17. Write down your answers. The starting point to solving any problem is to write down the questions and the answers.

3. THE NATURE OF MOTIVATION

Dictionaries define the word MOTIVE as 'moving or impelling power' or, 'form of mechanical energy used to drive machinery'. A motive is what induces a person to act. *Desire, fear* or simply *circumstance* are all examples of motive. To motivate, then, is to supply a motive, and motivation could be described as giving a person a reason for performing some action.

Motivation has both its negative and positive side and that observation leads me to make this very sweeping generality – the more intelligent a person is, the easier it is to motivate them – for motivation requires at least some degree of imagination and, in my experience, intelligence and imagination are closely linked.

The further down the intelligence ladder one moves, the more likely one is to encounter fear, insecurity and boredom – or, more precisely, people who, through a sufficient lack of imagination, have fallen into a depressing habit of claiming boredom as their almost perpetual state and private preserve.

In looking at the negative side of motivation, you may well ask where fear comes into this. Is fear an extreme example of ignorance – or could it be that ignorance is an extreme example of fear? Fear of the unknown; the insecurity that comes through a lack of knowledge and understanding – and once fear is in place, anger is only a few paces away. Fear born of ignorance is a dangerous emotion in an individual. It is all too easy to make false assumptions then, without allowing time to discover just how inaccurate those assumptions may be, it is easy to build on them until circumstances, through being so distorted, get completely out of hand – in fact, situations of this sort can often result in criminal behaviour and crimes of passion. But think of the dangers of this same syndrome when it happens on a group basis, 'Group Dynamics' is a fascinating study in itself. The way in which a crowd can assume an identity that is something right outside the normal behavioural pattern or experience of the individuals that make up that crowd, is an extraordinary phenomenon. Fear born of ignorance magnified through the multiplication of group dynamics can cause the collective emotion to reach epidemic and very frightening proportions. Classic examples, in this disturbed world of ours, are football hooliganism, race riots and other similar occurrences where fear, boredom or ignorance become the motivators.

Fear can take many forms. It is what often leads the under-achiever into deliberately seeking undemanding jobs because there is in that individual – possibly quite unconsciously – a fear of success. Alternatively, such a person may seek out very difficult jobs so that they cannot possibly be blamed if they eventually fail. Fear of success is often very deep-rooted and can be the result of unconscious and unresolved feelings of guilt prompted by the imagined possibility that they might better their father in some competitive sense.

All too frequently amongst young people one hears those tedious moans – 'it's b–o–r–i–n–g,' or 'I'm b–o–r–e–d'. These dull remarks are usually the resort of pretty dull people. The person who moans about being bored is unconsciously experiencing a lack of freedom because he/she **is no longer making the effort to choose or control the direction their life could and should take**. This attitude very often gives rise to a chain reaction of negative emotions, the outcome of which is to blame everything external for the state in which the individual perceives him or her self to be – yet never admitting or acknowledging the obvious fact that it is the individual's own attitude that is really at fault.

Young people – and we can see this particularly in areas of desperate unemployment – can create a breeding ground for negative thoughts and emotions as they collectively complain about the way the world is treating them, how rotten their parents are to them, how lousy their teachers at school are or were. They feed one another, piling negative upon negative, producing a thick dark cloud of demotivation that they allow to progressively envelop them, an emotional smoke-screen almost impossible to penetrate. Sadly, these youngsters may well carry the scars of their own negativism into later life and become part of that sad group of people who relish telling others how much they have suffered and what a bad hand life has dealt them.

That then is the nature of motivation in all its worst

forms. Those people who feel trapped by circumstances within a group of unfortunates, must isolate themselves from this negative and demotivational tide and try to decide how and why they have become sucked into the no-hope trap. Rarely will people admit that the blame for their circumstances lies within themselves – it is always outside agencies that have brought about their misfortunes. Once an individual can take a long, serious look at him or her self and realize that they are the cause of all their own effects, they are truly on the road to taking charge of their lives. They then have the opportunity to put that first foot forward at the start of a journey that could release all the wonderful, dormant potential that lies deep within them.

Positive action:

Ask yourself	1. How often have you given in to BOREDOM? – and what effect did it have on you?
	2. How often have you allowed yourself to be been pulled down by negative people?
	3. How often have you allowed yourself to feel it just wasn't worth bothering to do something that might have affected the quality of your life?
Resolve	1. Not to associate ever again with negative people.
	2. When you feel bored, seek out the cause or reason AND DO SOMETHING ABOUT IT!
	3. Don't allow yourself to be influenced by people you do not admire.
	4. Always try to maintain a positive attitude. There is no situation that does not have a possible positive solution.

4. ALL IN THE MIND

Our brain operates on two main levels – the conscious and the subconscious. These two states are in constant communication, one with the other, sorting, comparing, assessing, evaluating, decision-making. It is a curious partnership which, if it is to work as our servant and not our master, requires an understanding and appreciation of the manner in which this two-way flow operates. In very simplistic terms, *the subconscious will believe everything it is told!*

It has often been likened to a computer – indeed the computer is man's attempt to produce something as near the human brain as he can contrive – a device that will manipulate any information it is offered and supply feed-back to enable further decisions to be made or action to be taken.

If, for example, the subconscious receives the message 'I am so tired!' it will do everything to demonstrate and confirm the truth of this statement. It knows how and where to instantly find all the accumulated evidence of a lifetime, carefully and meticulously stored in the filing system, and is able to produce it so as to completely justify the statement with which it has been presented. Soon, not only are you feeling tired – real exhaustion begins to manifest itself, slowly bringing everything to a halt!

Capacity – or the degree to which you experience anything – is a state of mind. Tell yourself you are exhausted and you will be! But energy is always readily available when you decide to do whatever has to be done NOW! Thinking about the things you know you should have done is nothing more than an energy drain.

How often have you heard that saying 'if you want something done, ask a busy man'? Why should a busy man be the person to turn to? The answer is he is a NOW person, deriving his seemingly inexhausible supply of energy from immediate action. He is a person well aware of the value and benefit of never putting things off. The creed by which he lives his life is DO IT NOW! Putting things off until later is tantamount to giving our subconscious the chance to provide all the demotivational ideas that surround the concept of laziness. It is endowing the task with the label of 'unimportance'.

The unsuccessful person always has a great deal to say about why he hasn't done this or that – a whole book full of excuses. The successful person – the NOW person – doesn't tell you much at all. The job has been done so why waste time talking about it.

Attitude is so important and can effect everything we do, touching others just as easily as ourselves.

To become a NOW person rather than an IF or WHEN person requires only a minor change in attitude, a simple bit of fine-tuning in the way one approaches any task. If, for example, one is confronted with a task of fairly dramatic dimensions it is necessary to put the end result out of one's mind since that can so easily become the barrier to achievement. It is simply a question of getting down to the task immediately with the thought that, once started and dealt with in a business-like manner, it will very quickly be accomplished. Supposing one was faced with a 500 mile drive; nothing is gained by thinking what a long journey it is and of how tiring it is going to be or what a tedious chore it is. Too much energy is wasted that way. Rather it must be seen as a potentially enjoyable experience, breaking new ground, having plenty of time to think and observe whilst enjoying the actual act of driving. And, the sooner one gets into the car and starts, the sooner one will arrive. It is concentrating on the NOW and the HERE, not agitating oneself with anxious thoughts surrounding the outcome of what one is doing.

Take that old chore of army days, sitting before a mountain of potatoes that have to be peeled! It looks impossible. But if the job is approached in a relaxed way with the thought that it has to be done so one must aim to relax into it and get the maximum gain out of it by utilizing the time to think of better things, the job will get done systematically and almost unnoticed.

The whole point is that *things get done by **doing them** not by **thinking about them!*** Opportunities are grabbed up by the people who ask the question WHY? rather than those who are preoccupied by HOW? There is a vast world of difference between the attitudes embodied in these two small words. Abraham Lincoln put it well when he said . . . 'all good things come to those who wait – but only what's left behind by those who seize opportunities!'

I mentioned 'group dynamics' in the previous section; there is a curious example of collective attitude that emerges on a regular basis several times a year. Christmas, Easter and all Bank Holidays create a sort of national blockage for a week or so before each occasion. It is as though a barricade had been erected which we can see is blocking our path. The subconscious, being perpetually on its toes, is very quick to get wind of this and reacts by providing us with all the comparative, historic data to encourage the idea that there is little point in doing anything much until 'after the holiday' – an event that, in actuality, could have no possible bearing on this seeming need for immediate national lethargy. Millions of working hours must be lost each year in this grey that precedes all national holidays – and that is discounting the predictable absenteeism that follows every such event.

Extreme weather conditions bring on the same symptoms of national group time-wasting. Arctic conditions generate a type of larky enjoyment linked to what I call crisis-bonding – a situation in which people show a tendency to behave towards one another in ways that should be the norm rather than the unique. Everything comes to a halt – and not necessarily simply as the result of physical conditions. The subconscious is up to its tricks again. It produces a collective broadsheet of notions on these occasions, suggesting there is little point in trying to get to work in the happy anticipation of worsening conditions. Paradoxically, intrepid journeys have to be made on the basis of 'getting through' to indulge in an excess of panic food buying – natural preparation for, hopefully, an enforced stay-at-home. Everyone joins in the enjoyment of community misfortunes as pipes freeze, snow drifts have to be moved and crisis tea-making becomes the order of the day. The nation is now in an overdrive of group time-wasting, thoroughly enjoying every minute of crisis.

And the blame for all this bizarre behaviour must be laid squarely at the door of the subconscious in its innocent function of fuelling the fires with stimulating feedback.

All our thinking is composed of negatives and positives. The subconscious will accept either type of thought with equal enthusiasm and embrace it totally. It is not a reasoning machine – it merely acts on every instruction that is passed to it – and does this with breath-taking speed. It employs a filing system of staggering proportions and unlimited capacity. It is said that we only use about 5% of our total inherited potential as human beings. Einstein claimed that the average man only ever uses .02% of his intellectual capacity. And yet almost every word we have ever uttered, most sounds we have ever heard, every experience we have ever had, the bulk of everything we have ever seen or touched – all are recorded and all are instantly accessible. To say we have forgotten something is not strictly accurate – it is, if the information was originally stored, that we are having trouble with the mechanism of recall. The information is there – it's just winkling it out that presents the problem!

The mechanism of thinking, therefore, is a two-way traffic between our information gathering senses – seeing, feeling, hearing – and our subconscious which is constantly thumbing through the files recording, evaluating, comparing, to provide the instant feedback we need to guide and influence the next move. The brain, with its virtually unlimited storage facility, divides its function into long term storage and short term storage. People often marvel at the fact that they can remember things from years ago but have difficulty in recalling the most recent events. The short term storage facility is really nothing more than a note pad on which immediate information is scribbled. What is of real value is stored in the long term memory bank whilst the merely trivial is erased and forgotten. Like the computer, we have the 'save and continue' facility to ensure that nothing of value is lost.

A computer is a restless creature; as long as it is switched on, even though it is not being used, it is constantly checking and rechecking for anything it should be doing, anxious to be ready instantly for the next move. Similarly, even in sleep, the subconscious never ceases its activity. It is always ready to respond to any crumb of input that may be offered. It may at times appear to become confused – and this, I suspect, is the stuff of dreams.

The extraordinary images we experience in sleep happen, I believe, because the subconscious is always on duty and never actually closes down. The thinking, experiencing, every-day side of the mechanism is at rest and therefore not actually presenting anything much in the way of new material – the stuff of immediate experience – on which the subconscious can go to work. Odd, erratic thoughts and half-formed ideas flit across the mind, the subconscious picks up each and every one and provides the usual continuous service, the flow of comparative and informative feedback. It is as though a filing clerk is rushing around pulling information from the system in a completely haphazard and random way and presenting it for our inspection. Because of the inaccuracy of the stimulus, a lot of the resultant feed-back may have the appearance of utter nonsense. The sleeping mind accepts the images, adds its own embroidery and presents the subconscious with even more nonsense, the bizarre result – dreams and nightmares.

Any creative painter will tell you that the act of making a painting is not unlike a conversation. He is faced initially with a blank canvas on which he must make some form of mark as a starting point. Whatever this mark is, and wherever it is placed, says something back to him – some statement that will dictate what he should do next. His job is to listen and watch, respond to what the painting is saying to him. He may, of course, argue with what he sees. That is his prerogative. He makes further marks on the canvas and the process of discourse, statement and response, starts again. The true act of creation is a matter of listening, watching and responding – using the subconscious as a creative tool.

If, in our daily lives, we were to spend more time in listening to our subconscious and responding to its invaluable output, the benefits to us would be startling. But we must learn to listen. It is not always easy as the messages come thick and fast and are usually presented with disarming simplicity and un-canny accuracy. If we are not listening, so much of value can pass us by. We need to cultivate an attitude of belief in the value of what our subconscious presents to us and be prepared, through total trust, to act on the information.

We need to develop the courage of the partially sighted man who must – often for the sake of his own survival – always react immediately to what he *thinks* he sees. If he hesitates or stops to analyse or question the hazy images that instinct has interpreted, he could, at worst, be placing himself in great personal danger.

By listening to the inner voice and acting on its instructions we would improve our general efficiency, make better and more decisive judgements, enhance our relationships with others, experience the achieve-ment of our goals and ambitions more easily, and discover a greater fulfilment and enrichment in every aspect of our living.

The first step in this process is to eliminate negatives by learning to control negative thoughts without giving our subconscious the opportunity to demotivate us. It cannot do this of its own accord of course, for as we have seen, it has no intent, being merely a provider of the information necessary to the decision-making process.

We must learn that there is a danger in associating with negative people, for negativism, just like boredom, is a cancer which, given the right conditions in which to develop and flourish, will spread rapidly. Talking about negative things actually has a potential for incresing them by attracting more negatives into your life. There are some people – we have all met them – who always seem to have problems. Nobody else's worries are anything like theirs, indeed, they seem to have a sort of love affair with their problems, and a total reluctance to let go of them. No matter what the conversation, they will always manage to bring attention back to themselves and their perpetual, often imagined problems. Try not to associate with people like this – they are death to those with more ambitious aspirations and have the ability to infect whole groups of people. It is so easy for a group to produce a demotivational spiral down which each individual will slide far quicker than any one of them could ever manage on his or her own.

In the course of our daily lives we all accumulate a great deal of both mental and physical rubbish which we allow to surround us. This is just another form of negativism. Be bold! Eliminate everything from your life that makes no contribution to it! There is the greatest satisfaction in throwing out the irrelevant accumulation of junk! Go through your wardrobe and discard everything that you do not wear! We crowd and clutter our lives with so much rubbish, persuading ourselves that 'it might come in useful one day'. We know perfectly well that we are only delaying the day – which might be years ahead – when we will throw it away.

The point is that all the time we remain custodians of this extraneous burden, we are unconsciously being drained of energy through the sheer weight of its responsibility. Why else should we feel light-headed with delight and virtue when we have cast off the burden?

Just as your car needs servicing and your body needs exercise, so the brain enjoys being stretched and stimulated; to enable it to perform at peak capacity, it must be regularly serviced and exercised.

The brain – and you may find this rather surprising – uses language in its processes of storage and recall much more than it uses visual reference – the pictorial. It stands to reason, therefore, that the greater and more effective your grasp of language and its use, the more effective will be your mental functions. Just as your body requires stimulation to avoid becoming sluggish, your brain needs constant stretching to avoid stagnation. Read regularly to push your brain and exercise your intellect. Read the sort of material that you might normally shun as looking 'too difficult'. Not only will your vocabulary increase but your actual use of language will be enhanced. And the result? The depth and complexity of your thinking will increase in a direct ratio to the quality of the language you use and the breadth of your vocabulary.

The brain delights in and thrives on new experience, novelty and surprise, so deny it nothing in its quest for stimulation, fun, and exercise – this way you will never be demoralized or demotivated by your own boredom.

Positive action:
Believe in the amazing powers that are locked inside you. They are yours to use and control.

Try out your subconscious as a problem solver.
1. Write out your problem clearly in detail.
2. Try to solve it yourself as a first resort.
3. If you cannot see the answer, 'ask' your subconscious to resolve it for you. Pose the question and its alternatives clearly and concisely. Set a time limit for the answer – tomorrow morning or in 24 hours time.
4. Now FORGET THE PROBLEM COMPLETELY. There is no purpose in keeping a dog and barking yourself!

Be very aware of everything that passes through your mind. The answer is not going to come to you in letters of fire! 'Listen' in the silence for hunches, flashes of inspiration, sudden thoughts. These will often provide pointers to the solution. Believe strongly enough to ACT on what is suggested.

5. THE BEGINNINGS OF CHANGE

Each of us has always been – or so we like to think – the manager of our own affairs. We persuade ourselves that we are able to make of our lives anything we wish. This, generally speaking, is true, but how many of us are satisfied with the result? If we are seeking change it must be that we are not pleased with the way things have worked out so far. It could be that we have always tried to keep control of our lives as they progressed, rather than sincerely planning for the results we anticipate.

If we are to achieve change and improvement on a permanent basis, planning is the only positive way it can be brought about.

Change often begins with a general clear out! We have already talked about discarding the rubbish in our lives. The sheer sense of achievement that can be experienced by doing this makes a marvellous starting point. Not for nothing did that trite old saying 'a new broom sweeps clean' come about.

Standing on this spanking new and squeaky-clean launch platform, we must now decide on the nature of the changes we wish to bring about in both self and in the pattern of our life. Presumably success in some field is something for which we would all wish. True success in life is made up of so many elements. Acquiring a high degree of skill in performing some task satisfactorily is unlikely to represent true success. If this could be done whilst, at the same time, developing better relationships with our fellow humans, we might be getting closer to the real meaning of the word. My belief is that true success lies in a general expansion of all our talents and personal attributes following a sincere desire to not only enrich our own individual lives, but bring enrichment to the lives we touch as we travel towards the achievement of our personal goals.

This is what psychologists call the law of cause and effect. It is concerned with what we might call 'reciprocal action', or, as the Bible puts it, 'as ye sow so shall ye reap'.

What you get out of life will always be in direct ratio to the measure of what you put into it. Going back to our computer analogy, programmers are fond of the colourful adage 'crap in equals crap out!'

The way in which things have turned out for any of us in life is merely a reflection of how good or bad a manager we have proved to be. It is neither just or honest to place blame at any other door than our own! Once we stop blaming other people and circumstances for our own inadequacies and begin to understand the nature of responsibility, we hold a priceless key.

There is a theory that there is no such thing as mental

illness. What actually exists is a spectrum or scale, one end of which represents total irresponsibility, the other, responsibility. At the lower end lies the completely disturbed person whilst the top end we could assume to represent a totally normal mental state. Responsibility, looked at in this way, takes on a whole new meaning. Responsibility for our own actions and, since all our actions emanate from our thoughts, responsibility for the control of our mental processes.

Negative thoughts and emotions correspond to the individual's state of irresponsibility in varying degrees. But, what precisely are these negative emotions? Doubt, resentment, jealousy, guilt, envy – these are but a few. Every day of our lives we can easily reduce ourselves to the state of temporary cripples with these negatives as we go through the motions of self-pity, anger, resentment and blame. It is, of course, our old friend the subconscious going about its impartial work, helping to fan the flames through the process of assessment and feed-back. Whilst we would mostly wish to rid ourselves of these poisonous elements, we go out of our way to justify them – until, that is, we begin to realize that we DO have some degree of control over our own thought processes.

Negative emotions are actually difficult to sustain for very long unless we can continue the tedious process of justification by explaining our negatives to others, thereby keeping the embers glowing – and incidentally demotivating our unfortunate victims in the process. If we are to rid ourselves of justification we must develop an attitude of neutrality by aiming to become, ultimately, completely non-judgmental. Only this way can we stop negative emotions from developing and halt the process that allows our subconscious, through its natural and entirely innocent function, to generate that dangerous condition of unwanted, negative energy that can so easily become quite destructive.

There is an interesting experiment anyone can try – and the outcome will be surprisingly beneficial. Make a declaration between yourself and your partner that neither will criticize the other for a period of 90 days! If either party breaks the pact, they go back to the start of a new 90 day period. You will be surprised at the result, once a few false starts have inevitably been made. Try it! – see what it does for your relationship and for your own self-image.

We often imagine, and, indeed, like to persuade ourselves, that negative emotions are the result of external circumstances – they are not. Rather, they are the result of our response to those circumstances and the more we allow ourselves to justify our emotions, the more we are fanning the flames until we create a situation of our own devising that is capable of consuming us. If we can stop justifying everything we have the chance to disengage ourselves from emotional involvement, turn our backs on the situation, and walk away from it unscathed.

Positive action
What about that declaration between partners?
Why not try it – and watch what happens!

6. TAKING CONTROL

Plato, the great Athenian philosopher, said: 'The first and best victory is to conquer self. To be conquered by self, is of all things, the most shameful and vile.'

Obviously, in the quest for change and development, the making of decisions is of vital importance. But decisions must be decisive. It is, for example, no use at all saying to yourself 'I think if I really tried I could stop smoking.' A statement of this sort already has provisional failure built into it. It is devoid of commitment, has no time scale and totally lacks real conviction. Your sub-conscious would have a heyday with a remark like that!

If on the other hand you said 'I will stop smoking as of *now*!', there is nothing more to be said! The job is done, the commitment made. It is simply not possible to partially stop smoking – you either smoke or you don't. The decision is total and final. A decision with possibilities built into it is no decision at all. The only built-in factor must be commitment.

That kind of decision, based on commitment and total belief in its result has a way of causing events. If you decide what you want (desire) and force yourself to take some appropriate action, you are creating the momentum to achieve a result. This is all part of the mechanism of what I have called 'the human dynamo' – the success-breeds-success syndrome.

The subconscious through its constant evaluation and assessment function is your in-built decision maker. The mechanism is yours to control but, before that can happen, any previously imposed controls that govern attitudinal and behavioural patterns that are detrimental must be removed – the obvious influence of parents and teachers as well as the less obvious such as television and advertising. Too often these preconditional influences cause unconscious worry, even confusion as the individual imposes unnecessary restraints and controls by anticipating the future even before any conscious decision has been made. The result of this can be that we often leave undone some of the things that should have been done and do things we do not truly want to do.

Choice is always there! We have the choice to go on being influenced by past conditioning or we can take control of the decision making mechanism and thereby master the possibility for change.

It is inevitable for any of us that we will make bad decisions from time to time. What we must avoid at all costs is developing a *fear* of making bad decisions. Look on bad decisions as things from which you can learn and develop. Life cannot be all 'ups' – there must be 'downs' too. Where, after all, have you come from when you are experiencing an up? It is the downs in life that make the ups possible – even inevitable. So, learn and profit from poor decisions you may have made – you will rarely make the same mistake again.

If life has knocked you to the bottom you have the choice to either stay there and wallow in destructive self-pity, or make the conscious choice to do something about your plight. Making a decision of that sort with all the commitment you can muster will kick start the process of rebirth and revival – after all, the only way is up! It can bear being said once more – any journey, no matter how long, starts with just one step.

Making decisions is a long way from being the same thing as stating preferences. The difference is that between *expectation* and *wishing*. Far too many people, in making what they think is a positive decision, spend too much time thinking about how the result can be achieved. The decision must be based on WHY, not on HOW. Once the decision is made, the necessary immediate action is what will generate the energy to answer the HOW question.

So the process is:
1. Decision (based on expectation and the desire for a result)
2. Immediate action (commitment)
3. Heightened awareness to recognize the 'how' when it reveals itself.

True decision taking requires guts and courage because the degree of commitment necessary to trigger all the magic offers no half measures. Any committed decision has a wonderful finality about it that is its ultimate guarantee of successfully producing the desired result. Decisions of this sort leave total satisfaction and a great sense of relief in their wake.

Successful business men are making vital, committed decisions every day. Decisions they stand by, decisions on which they are prepared to stake their reputation. And yet, to the same man, many personal decisions are extremely difficult. How can such a forceful and dynamic man say he can't stop smoking? The answer is simple – *he doesn't want* to stop. There is no real desire to produce the commitment and trigger the action.

Desire for change must precede commitment to action.

Decision making is a skill and like all skills improves with practice. It is always easier to put off a decision than it is to make one. Too many people drift through life allowing others to make decisions for them. The result is a loss of initiative and drive allowing for flabby attitude to develop from which it is all too easy to place one's own failure or lack of thrust on someone else's doorstep thereby side-stepping all personal responsibility.

Self-esteem is all-important to every one of us. It is greatly enhanced through the satisfaction that comes from making life-changing decisions with the commitment to see them through until the goal is reached.

Most of us have become lazy about making decisions and revert too easily to wishing for rather than to making the effort to face up to the courage required to produce committed decisions. If real change is to take place, this state of inertia must be overcome. **Decision making is the key to taking control of your life**. A decision is only worthwhile if it results in action – and action brings about change. And change will defeat the state of inertia which is the greatest stumbling block to self-improvement and advancement.

Inertia – which can embody both boredom and self-pity – is the stagnating enemy that lurks within each one of us, waiting and watching for the opportunity to drag us into a state of sluggish and blunted lifelessness. The dictionary defines the state of inertia as 'sloth' – and is that not one of the seven deadly sins?

Our greatest weapon against this sleazy adversary is the realization of its damaging potential. Action and activity are the weapons to employ – taking control, being a decision-maker and taker.

So, the choice is ours – whether to become angry and petulant or calm and reasonable. When things are not going the way we feel they should, we can decide not to apportion blame – the worst of all negative emotions. There is a simple and yet supremely powerful thought we can hold in the conscious mind and repeat to ourselves whenever negative emotions begin to show signs of getting the upper hand:

'I AM RESPONSIBLE'

Try it! It is actually difficult, whilst repeating this

simple phrase, to maintain truly negative thoughts and emotions and keep them alive. 'I am responsible!' You will quickly realize that this is the key to ridding yourself of so much that is not worth holding on to. You are the captain of your own destiny, the vessel for which you are totally responsible – it is up to you to always keep a firm hand on the tiller!

The outcome of the 1992 General Election saw the Labour Party blaming the Conservatives, but even more so, the Press, for their defeat. There seemed little awareness of the simple fact that the responsibility for their defeat lay with themselves. Either they failed to present themselves to the electorate as a sufficiently attractive proposition, or they would not face up to the possibility that the country did not want a socialist government. However one looks at it, they were responsible for the circumstances of their own downfall. This failure to accept responsibility added nothing to the party image. As time goes by they will most certainly feel a need to accept the facts and assume the much needed mantle of responsibility for themselves. Only then can their fortunes begin to change.

I would like to suggest that if there is but one thing you remember after reading this book, 'I am responsible' should be it. It is a tiny phrase worthy of considerable thought and reflection. It comes remarkably close to attaining the status of possessing the key to all of life.

Once you realize and, more importantly, believe that external circumstances cannot touch or harm you emotionally, you are truly in charge – you are indeed responsible!

'Belief' is perhaps the most potent and dynamic word in the English language. Belief is the 'magic' ingredient of success. Intelligence and ability are certainly necessary – but it is belief that can carry you to the farthest and most exciting areas of life. It can demolish barriers, break down restrictions and allow one to travel just as far as one wants to go. With belief, all things are possible, all doors open.

Sportsmen and women are a splendid example of the effects of belief in action. At the highest levels in sport, where events are won or lost on the basis of fractions of a second, mental preparation – to tune the subconscious to the winning attitude – is of vital importance, not even allowing the tiniest doubt to creep in. The competitor's performance is rehearsed over and over in the mind so that the whole scenario of winning is firmly implanted in the subconscious. This is indeed belief of an amazingly high order.

Golf and snooker are two examples of games that are played to a large extent in the mind. As a spectator, it is fascinating to watch the domination of the game swinging back and forth between the players as psychological advantages boost and demoralize each player in turn. When one player is on top all things are possible and it is easy to observe how the positive attitudes of certainty and expectation have taken control. The opponent, on the other hand, can be seen demonstrating all the opposite emotions as he begins to make minor mistakes as attitudes become less positive and a general demoralization takes hold.

The subconscious, being the recipient and guardian of all previous experience can be both a help and a hinderance since it will produce all the emotions that surrounded both victory and defeat on previous occasions. It is possible for the world-class player to develop a situation through which the really big prizes constantly elude him and he suffers a run of merely second place achievements. This is a mould that can be very difficult to break. Assuming he is at least as good as, if not actually better than, his opponent, at the point where victory seems to be within the players grasp, the subconscious is likely to produce a play-back of the undermining feelings from past events. Only the strongest mental attitudes can overcome this situation. There must be total belief in the fact that coming second is a thing of the past. The player must be certain of his emotions and the *desire* to win is of paramount importance. Only the winning position will do and the sportsman's mental preparation must be good enough to impress all these attitudes on his subconscious so that, rather than eroding motivation at the crucial point, it actually produces a surge of positive inspiration at the right moment, strong enough to put victory in the player's hands. There is a fascinating two-way flow in the sheer electricity generated in a high-powered game. It is a battle of motivational domination, not just brilliant play, as the participants sense who is on top and who is the under-dog.

Belief comes in many forms:
* belief in oneself
* belief in what one is doing and in one's ability
to do it
* belief in others and in their abilities
* belief in the strength of one's thoughts and in the
peaks of one's possible achievement

Human beings respond gloriously to their own effort. The greater the effort – and therefore the resultant generated energy – the more their interest is stimulated. They stop making excuses for their situation and begin to realize the value of conditions such as freedom, happiness, enthusiasm, joy and the excitement of commitments. Interest in what one is doing, in its turn, produces its own kind of energy, but it is effort that fires it, and hey presto! – we have created that 'moving or impelling power' that the dictionary defined.

Positive action:

1. Repeat to yourself – but aloud – at least 10 times
   a day: 'I AM RESPONSIBLE!'
   Remember it when ever there is a tendency to
   blame others or to blame circumstances for
   something that you feel is not right.
2. Try to set at least two goals each day. Nothing
   too dramatic. They may only be small things but,
   in the achievement of them, you will have been
   lead into positive action of one sort or another.
3. Try to cultivate the habit of thinking in terms of
   'Why' rather than 'How' when faced with problems or the need for decisions. The WHY route
   will usually provide the answers you are seeking.
   The HOW route is all too often a cul-de-sac.

7. TURNING THINGS AROUND

It is not an uncommon thing for anyone to feel depressed. The effect, though, is usually very demotivating. Demotivation can be like entering a downward spiral which, if left unchecked, carries one lower and lower until a situation develops which is very difficult to reverse.

Depression often has the effect of forcing us inside ourselves and allowing us to wallow in self-pity, remorse, dissatisfaction, feelings of injustice, indeed the entire gamut of negative emotions that are most destructive to human well-being. I am sure, having read this far, you must be very aware of the process that is causing these dramatic effects. The subconscious is at work again! It is of course quite unfair to berate it as it operates in total ignorance of the results its actions may cause, it is merely conscientiously performing its job of providing all the information needed to justify the statements made to it. Try then only to have positive thoughts and never to let your subconscious know you are depressed if you feel you cannot cope with the inevitable result! Being aware of just what can happen – what the process entails – we must aim not to allow ourselves to slide too far down that spiral of demotivation.

At this very low ebb, the likelihood of being able to produce the degree of effort necessary to haul oneself back up the spiral is remote – but certainly not impossible.

Difficult as it may be, there is one sure way to overcome such a deep and devastating level of demotivation. When the subject least feels like it, the only hope lies in raising their level of activity dramatically and swiftly – for lower down lies irresponsibility, loss of control and a disintegration of inner self. Yes, this all sounds very dramatic and perhaps over exaggerated – it is not. These things are happening every day.

When it has to be produced, the effect of a sudden burst of activity, is like push-starting a car. The sheer drama of making the supreme effort will produce the degree of electricity necessary to excite and stimulate the subject until he is really motoring again, and enjoying the excitement that his own endeavour has promoted.

A really active salesman will tell you that during a working week he can become progressively more and more motivated by his own efforts until, by Friday, he is so highly charged he almost resents the fact that a weekend has arrived and is about to bring a halt to his relentless and ever-mounting state of excitement! However, without the weekends to act as the safety valve – necessary to the release of the powerful head of steam he has built up – he would create a self-destruct situation and simply explode! Crisis, stress and all the attendant problems would certainly be the outcome.

Fortunately, it is not possible to maintain such a high degree of self-motivation. Motivational peaks have a real value but peaks are only points of transcience, they are not places of residence! The level of motivation needed to attain a peak cannot be maintained for very long.

One of the most exciting aspects of human life is contrast. If we were always at the zenith of achievement, there would be peaks no longer. How can we recognize the arrival at a peak unless we experience the troughs that lie on either side? It is this contrast that makes our journey exciting and worthwhile, for nothing is truer than that to travel hopefully is often better than to arrive. Hope, expectation and optimism are the most sustaining of human emotions; without these life would indeed be a drab affair. People who claim boredom as their special preserve, live without allowing these emotions to touch them, and are the poorer for it . . .

The peaks and troughs of motivational activity, are vital to the existence of imaginative and creative people, providing the current that keeps the human dynamo humming. There are occasions, however, when the experience is too dramatic. Pop singers are prime examples of this phenomenon. During a live performance they rise through all the levels of excitement at great speed, drawing their stimulation from the feedback their audience provides. As they in turn stimulate the audience still further, 'group dynamics' takes over and a vast collective energy is generated, something far beyond the bounds of any single individual. By the end of the performance, this collective energy dissipates and is, as it were, shared out between the individual members of the audience who carry it away with them. The unfortunate performer, however, is left high and dry, adrenalin thundering through his system and nothing on which to expend it. His mood begins to change, modified by these altered circumstances: scientists, no doubt, would explain this as a chemical adjustment taking place within the bodily system. Denied the necessary stimulation of his audience, the performer is left to face the problem of his lonely descent from this 'high'. It is not difficult to understand how drugs, for some people in such circumstances, offer the chance of staying on the peak that took so much energy to attain.

Yes, motivation is a tremendous power in our lives – the greatest difficulty we face is in turning the tap on and off at will, achieving the peaks when we need them most. A highly motivated person, responding to the excitement level that has been achieved, is a very magnetic being to whom others are easily and naturally drawn. People love to deal and associate with successful people.

A friend of mine who has been a professional painter for many years has always been fascinated by a pattern of events that he noticed kept on recurring in his working life. To make a good living as a painter it is necessary for him to have at least three exhibitions a year. Galleries of the calibre in which he usually exhibits, plan all their exhibitions well in advance, and so my friend is always aware of his commitments at any time for two or three years ahead. His year, therefore, is divided by three or four natural deadlines towards which he is always working. He knows how many pictures will be needed for each exhibition and so he can plan his work to coincide with the dead-lines which will inevitably occur roughly every three or four months.

Each period starts slowly then begins to gather its own natural momentum – a reflection of the painter's mounting excitement – the natural outcome of the creative process. As a deadline approaches (the date on which all the paintings must be finished, framed and ready to be shipped out to the exhibition venue) the excitement increases in proportion to the time scale piling on the pressure. Eventually a massive peak is reached – a culmination of creative satisfaction and achievement, spiked with the adrenalin the process has injected. At this point my friend is on a 'performance high' and not really wanting the process to stop. But this is when odd things begin to happen . . .

In the normal course of events he doesn't have many visitors to his studio as most of his work is sold through galleries. And yet every time he reaches this emotional plateau, he can be certain of one thing – the telephone will start to ring and people he has never heard of will ask whether he has any paintings in the studio that they could come and see!

You might think, as he did at first, that there was a very useful and usable system at work – but it would only work if the pattern could be relied on. It should, in theory, be possible to sell the majority of the paintings without them ever leaving the studio, cutting out the middle man and any need to pay away hefty commissions on each sale!

Fortunately my painter friend resisted any such thoughts, attractive as the temptation was to him. He was well aware that it was the gallery bookings and the imposed deadlines that produced the peaks of motivational excitement required to make the magic work.

This might seem fanciful stuff, but we are dealing here – yet again – with the power of the subconscious mind. There is a kind of magic that only occurs through thought concentration which operates on the basis that whatever you think, believe in and concentrate upon, will grow . . . The implication is not simply that the object of concentration grows merely in our subconscious – it will actually emerge, in tangible form, into our reality. Thought energy, fuelled and accelerated by acute excitement has the power to draw people in sympathy with you into your life.

Positive action:
1. Try always to maintain very positive thoughts and observe the effects your attitude can have on your surroundings and the people whith whom you come in contact.
2. Always expect the best of life and believe yourself to be worthy of receiving an abundance of life's good things.

8. RECOGNITION AND REWARD

As we have already seen, it is possible to motivate oneself by sheer activity and benefit from the stimulating cycle that naturally follows on from it. But, to produce real peaks of motivational excitement, we must have something to aim for, a point in time that represents arrival and achievement. Arrival may not be the most exciting or satisfying event, even at times being a disappointment – but the important factor is that a point of arrival provides the reason and stimulus for the journey having taken place.

Goals and targets, then, are necessary parts of the motivational process. Achievement is a great stimulus, reward offers confirmation of achievement and provides the most important of all human needs – recognition.

If you were to ask the majority of people what they thought was the greatest motivator, the answer would almost certainly be money. They would be wrong! Money is a motivator to the person who hasn't got any but, assuming we are considering the motivation of someone who has reasonable earnings, dangling the financial carrot isn't necessarily very effective. Despite what I have just said, earning a lot of money is obviously motivational – but the real reward is being SEEN to have have earned a lot of money!

Recognition is the single most rewarding, and therefore motivational, aspect of all human endeavour – the real and lasting motivator in a competitive environment where winning (more of this later) is mistakenly seen to be the only measure of real achievement. However, being seen to succeed is of immense value to us all.

The painter, the writer, the inventor, and anyone who produces anything that relies for its success on the tangible appreciation of others, gets recognition (and therefore reward) through natural feedback. This may be in the form of critical appraisal or simply – and more practically – through sales. Feedback is elemental to the creative process; it is what keeps the fire burning. Without this recognition the creative process would whither and die as nobody can work effectively in total isolation for any length of time.

Recognition then is a strong motivator. But there are two sides to every coin. Demotivation, is the result of what we perceive as being seen to have failed.

In their anxiety to see their children succeed, parents often make the unfortunate mistake of underestimating the importance of recognition. Children thrive on having their achievements noticed and commented on. Parents are so often too critical in their understandable wish to see their child shine, not realizing what a destructive effect this can have when all the child is hoping for is a kindly pat on the head. At worst, the over critical parent can actually stifle talent. Sometimes in adult life people experience vague feelings of inadequacy and this can almost certainly be attributed to a lack of parental understanding of fundamental needs.

Another, often unaccountable inherited emotion takes the form of a vague sense of 'fear' – a feeling of unease or apprehension for which there seems no immediate reason when we are confronted by specific tasks or events. These feelings are almost certainly rooted in repressed emotions – again bequeathed to us by parents in their total innocence. Being told as a child that 'you never seem to do anything right', or confronted with questions such as 'why are you always so clumsy?', 'why can't you tell the truth?', 'why don't you ever learn?' all left their mark as these concepts became the possession of the sub-conscious. Everything has been filed away, seemingly 'forgotten', lying dormant deep down in the filing system as 'fear factors'. They have a habit of emerging as strangely disturbing sensations when matching circumstances to those to which they originally referred confront us, usually producing those resultant feelings of inadequacy for which we cannot rationally account.

One of the purposes of this book is to create an awareness of feelings of this nature and then to provide a means of 'dismantling' them so they may be replaced by a more positive self-image. Such a change will almost certainly be instrumental, through the removal of 'blocks', in allowing you to be the success you feel you could or should be.

Negative emotions are something that children just do

not have from birth. They are spontaneous and completely uninhibited. Babies' emotions are utterly straight forward; they cry when they are sad and laugh when they are happy. Children learn by watching, so, from the often unconscious examples of adults, they can develop negative emotions and habits which stay with them throughout life. As adults they have the opportunity to do something to regain this lost inner control.

Children have a wonderful natural talent for all things creative. They are blessed with an uncluttered, honest view of the world about them – a gift granted to all of us in equal measure. Parents and schools, often quite unwittingly, undermine and destroy this gift by imposing on the child the concept that 'adults know best'. Maybe the time has come to get rid of the idea that age, in some mysterious way, bestows wisdom!

Children, left alone, will produce marvellous, un-inhibited drawings but, all too often, teachers, not perhaps fully understanding the process they are watching, cannot resist intervening – 'teaching' this natural creative talent out of the child. Successful creative painters are simply those who have managed to resist the teaching process and thereby preserved their natural gift more or less intact.

Children are born fearless and brimful of natural curiosity which leads them on to explore and investigate the world that surrounds them. Adults are usually quick to react, to reprimand – reactions often born out of fear or apprehension for the child's safety. But these constant warnings to 'leave that alone', 'don't touch!', 'come down from there!' only serve to give the child the feeling that every time it steps outside its boundaries, it gets punished – or at least told off. Eventually, this repetitious behaviour manifests itself in adult life as fear of failure – a conditioned reflex from the childhood pattern of authoritarian criticism.

As a classic example of not understanding the need for recognition, the school report takes a lot of beating! 'Could do better'! The child to whom that is applied may have been, in their own way, making a supreme effort and all they needed to stimulate them was a modicum of praise and recognition to encourage them to greater efforts. The comment 'could do better' is a sad put-down that does actually suggest not much effort has been made at all.

In this small, seemingly trivial example lies one of the real secrets of success. The cumulative effect of all these remarks and attitudes has, in all probability, produced our own measure of self-esteem – the value we place on our perception of ourselves. Quite possibly the child could do better but simply telling it that achieves very little. Far better if the teacher had recognized that the child had actually achieved certain goals, no matter how trivial these may have been. There would then have been something positive that would have meant so much to the child. The parents would have reacted in a positive manner and given the child a tremendous boost to reinforce the teacher's assessment. There would have been benefit to everyone! More importantly, the child's self-esteem would have remained intact and even been strengthened. It could then have been set new goals, new levels of achievement at which to aim, and these would have been both stimulating and motivational.

Reward for achievement fulfils yet another important human requirement – it reinforces achievement by means of tangible recognition. Reward can be a matter of 'contract' – 'clean your shoes and I'll give you a sweet!' That is reward directly related to a required action – little more than a bribe, in fact. That form of reward can obviously have an ongoing reaction. The shoes don't get cleaned unless the sweet is offered!

In the world of sales an obvious example of the contract reward is the Overseas Sales Convention – an extravaganza – as guests of the employer – in some exotic venue.

Now this can have various effects:

1. To some the qualification is so far beyond their reach they consider it unattainable, so make no effort. The outcome is probably progressive mediocrity terminating in failure.
2. To some the achievement of the qualification is inevitable, producing, at best, a smug satisfaction and a blase acceptance of the reward.
3. To those who almost made the qualification in the previous year, the reward is definitely motivational. They are not going to miss out again.
4. As the year of qualification progresses, those seen to be on course will certainly be stimulated to

strive harder, particularly as the dead-line draws near.

It is vitally important that the contracted reward, especially when the period of qualification has been protracted, is of the very highest standard and quality. If it falls short or even hints at economy or cost-cutting, its value will be totally negated, and the promoter will be forever discredited.

So, the contract reward, although perhaps a little artificial, has its place but also its pitfalls and dangers.

Any individual can use the concept of contract reward for behavioural modification very effectively on a purely personal basis. Having set a goal you might also contract yourself to receive a 'prize' or reward such as a meal out – or anything that represents some form of particular enjoyment – when the goal is achieved. It can be very useful to actually write out the contract as a means of reinforcement and of endowing it with greater value. By way or example, if the aim was to give up smoking, the contract could have progressive rewards built into the programme, in recognition of continued achievement. It is important that the reward is something really appreciated to give it maximum motivational value. The contract too, can be used as an undisguised bribe through denial – 'no more beer until you have cut the grass!', or, 'no television until you have finished your homework!' The greatest reward in terms of psychological satisfaction comes through recognition – being seen to have achieved and having that achievement publically recognized. The simple act of the head of a department walking up to someone in front of his or her peers and telling them what a fine job they have done, could be of inestimable value to that person – especially if the remarks are accompanied by some form of physical contact, maybe nothing more than a hand laid on the shoulder. The pleasure this provokes is yet another manifestation of childhood programming – a strong need for touching and, particularly in the formative years, the need for a lot of love involving touching. We really are strange creatures, aren't we! But, having an understanding of some of these basic patterns of behaviour can have great value in helping us modify and adjust our inherited behavioural habits to advantage.

Positive action:

1. If you are a parent, try to remember what it was like to be a child. Try not to frustrate your own children and try to avoid always wanting to show them HOW! Most people, including children, have no objection to being told *what to do* – but most of hate being told *how to do it*. This simply denies initiative.

2. Always praise good deeds publically. Always deliver reprimands in private.

3. Cultivate the habit of being more outgoing – and don't be afraid to *touch* people!

9. FALSE LIMITATIONS

Many people have grown up with an idea of themselves that is, quite possibly, wildly inaccurate. They are in danger of being severely limited by a self-image that doesn't begin to suggest what their true potential might be.

The limitations we place on ourselves because of what we perceive as an inadequate self-image, may be completely false and without justification. It is, therefore, most important that we examine our own self-image and question whether the persona we have built up over the years is the real person – the person we truly feel ourselves to be. Nothing need be accepted simply because it is 'there'. As we have seen, circumstances and influences can have produced behavioural patterns that are actually obscuring the true personality. We must be bold enough to question everything – ask yourself this simple question – **is being you really good enough? And are you comfortable with YOU?**

An inadequate self-image can easily produce feelings of guilt and inferiority – feelings for which it is often difficult to account – endowing a person with a vague idea that they don't deserve good things to happen to them. Earlier I mentioned destructive criticism and the effect it can have on a developing child. In adult life the result of this can emerge as a 'fear' of success and an uneasy feeling of 'unworthiness'. The tendency, under these circumstances, is to write-off success as merely luck or chance and to experience extreme discomfort and dis-ease at any public revelation of it.

There is a simple technique for dispelling these intrusive attitudes which we will come to in due course.

'I'll try . . .' is the precursor to one of the greatest of false limitations. It is pre-empting failure by the implied negativism built into the phrase. 'I'll try to catch the 6.30 train,' It is virtually tantamount to declaring that you will miss it! These are simply examples of making excuses for possible failure in advance. If you don't mean something, don't say it!

We have inherited so many limitations through the lessons of upbringing. Quite irrational fears have so often been imposed upon us and will limit what we can achieve. A classic example of this can be demonstrated by placing a six foot length of timber, six inches wide, on the floor and asking someone to walk along it. This they can do without the slightest worry or consideration, even making a joke of the simplicity of your request. But place the two ends of the timber on a couple of chairs and ask the same person to do it again! Many people will find it impossible, even though the timber is only a couple of feet above the floor. For those that can walk along the timber, position it even higher. There will be a height at which nobody will willingly walk along it! It is the same piece of timber, the same width – all that has changed is its position.

Every one of us is bound by the limitations of experience and early training, only exploiting a fraction of our real potential, not just because we are fearful, but because we are basically lazy,.

Many people exist within their own particular comfort zones and are far too easily satisfied with a relatively low threshold of wealth and general standards to be bothered to make any great effort. And yet they will still grumble without knowing what it is that their life lacks. Every human being needs to strive for something, to have some sort of goal or target – but the comfort zone is an ever-lurking danger to us all. The cosy glow of relative success can stifle further ambition, putting it on the shelf, as it were, until we feel like making another effort to take the next step. Ah, such delusion! Once inside the comfort zone, the state of happy euphoria it generates will almost certainly keep us there. It imposes its own brand of restriction by maintaining feelings of satisfaction at the semi-achieve-ment it really represents.

Our confidence depends so much on not feeling restricted and in knowing that our achievements are observed and recognized by both our peers and superiors. To be seen to be successful, even in a relatively small way, is of tremendous motivational value, and each time we can repeat the experience, the feelings of self-esteem are amplified and strengthened. These experiences are the building bricks of personal growth and achievement.

It is rare for real change to be achieved in giant strides. It usually occurs as a slow process of regularly repeated incidents and a conscious persistence. This is the 'I WILL' of self-motivation and it is imperative not to let up until success is achieved.

One of the common mistakes constantly perpetuated by senior management in large organizations is to assume that because a good performer appears to 'have arrived' he is no longer in need of praise and recognition but will slog on indefinitely, happily performing his tasks with ability and dedication. How wrong this concept is! And how deeply damaging.

The time will inevitably arrive when the employee begins to question his value to the organization, speculating on whether his superiors are even aware of what a good job he is doing. Silence, on the part of management, may simply arise out of their total satisfaction, yet, at the same time, demonstrating a sad lack of understanding of the employee's basic needs. But unless the employee is made aware of management attitudes, his doubts begin to multiply and become tinged with disappointment and disillusion through this assumption that his abilities are not fully appreciated.

Sometimes, of course, disregard of the need for recognition is coupled with a fear on the part of management that the employee is becoming too good at his job and could be posing a threat – but here we are getting into a whole new subject!

In the process of self-examination and self-appraisal try to identify the areas of false limitation.

What is holding you back?
What are your in-built fears?
Are you sitting in a comfort zone of your own making?
If you feel you are – what are the factors that have created it?

Remember – **once an enemy is identified it becomes so much easier to defeat.**

Positive action:
1. If you are an employer or manager, develop the habit of recognizing achievement in others. This applies at all levels – and you cannot do it too often. *Everyone* needs recognition, no matter how far up the ladder they are. It is the thing that will always bring out the best in people. It is what *corporate loyalty* is made of.
2. Ask yourself if you are existing in a comfort zone. If you think you are, set new goals and strive towards new achievement.
   Stretch yourself at all times and aim for something just out of reach.

10. WINNERS AND LOSERS

Any journey, no matter how long, starts with just one step. It is the same for all of us and yet there will always be those who arrive first, having completed the journey more easily than others, and travelled what seemed to be a different, simpler route. These people appear to be natural winners whilst others seem always to get left far behind.

Are we divided into winners and losers? Is there something, some magic thing, that successful people do, or something they know or possess that evades the remainder of the world? Could it be luck? Could it be that certain people get all the opportunities whilst others are left out in the cold?

It is easy to identify successful people in all walks of life. It is not that they are better at what they do than the next man – it is that something about them ensures that they are perceived as achievers.

They are taken notice of – they are successful because they believe that to be their natural state!

They can see no reason why they should not succeed.

They do not place stumbling blocks of their own making in the path or even consider for a moment that they cannot succeed.

They visualize themselves as successful and expect nothing less!

Those four statements express a particular feeling – successful people have a very highly developed sense of self-esteem. They have good feelings about themselves, they like themselves and are aware both of that as a very necessary ingredient to success and achievement as much as the need to consciously develop a strong and agreeable self-image. Another thing of which most successful people are aware is their personal uniqueness. Each individual is totally unique. There has never been anyone like him or her before and there will never be anyone like him or her again. It is strange that so many people are content to ignore this in their wish to be absorbed into the mass of humanity where they can be contentedly anonymous. These are the naturally unambitious members of society who will never do anything particularly exciting or remarkable despite the fact that, if in some way we could touch their 'hot button', they might be galvanized into the sort of action that could change their lives. Their special problem is that they have such a low level of self-esteem that they are unable to visualize themselves in any kind of sucessful situation.

All successful people have decided what they want out of life. However, there is something of which they are all aware – they know that all success has its price and that no achievement comes without effort, dedication to an idea, and willing sacrifice. Luck, should it come into the equation, is purely a bonus. Almost certainly any 'luck' will only have been the result of hard work and the ability to quickly recognize opportunity.

Motivation and success are interchangeable entities and cross-fertilize one another. Motivation normally has to precede success since it is the driving force that leads towards it. But – and we are back to that magic which powers the human dynamo – motivation can also be the product of success, stimulating and pushing one forward to even greater achievements and their attendant rewards.

We all have choice! It is for us to decide whether we have success or failure – and it is far easier to fail!

Nobody really knows what they are made of until they extend themselves towards a higher achievement than they have so far experienced. The more people attempt to push back the frontiers of human endeavour, the more they discover the latent capabilities of their own potential.

There was a time, not so many years ago, when it was unthinkable that man could run a mile in four minutes. Roger Bannister truly believed it was possible and that, with the aid of his friends, he was the man capable of proving it. As we know, he did it. He achieved what seemed then to be the impossible. Because a new benchmark had been estabished, others recognized and accepted the challenge, pushing the frontiers of achievement back even further, creating new records, new targets.

On the day Queen Elizabeth II was crowned. Edmund Hillary reached the top of Everest with Sherpa

Tensing – a truly remarkable achievement. Yet, on one day in May 1992, 37 people did the same thing, representing several separate expeditions!

Achievements of the calibre that both Bannister and Hillary demonstrated come only through total self-belief and faith in one's own ability. Never be put off by failure – failure is not there to show you cannot do something, but to demonstrate where you went wrong and what must be adjusted so that achievement of that particular goal becomes possible. Take the example of the professionl footballer. For every goal he scores he may have made up to a dozen attempts which failed. Every shot at goal was expected to find its mark but he knows that to score every time is just not possible. If he allowed his mistakes and inaccuracies to get him down, he would not last for very long in the game. He has learned to make positives out of his negatives. Each missed shot increases his determination to succeed – and he does.

Learn to turn adversity to your own advantage. The ugly duckling did, after all, find it was a swan! Shakespeare, as always, put it so well – 'Sweet are the uses of adversity, which like the toad, though ugly and venomous, wears yet a precious jewel in its head.'

It is common practice at motivational seminars, of which I have attended my fair share, to present super-sports personalities as examples of true achievement and as *winners* to be emulated.

Bannister's attainment on the running track was real success, motivated in the right way through a genuine desire for the achievement of a very personal goal. By contrast, the super-sportsman or woman is only a winner because, in the process of their achievement, someone else has had to be a loser. Achievement in sport is so often held up as a splendid example of preparation for even greater success in life. Has anyone really achieved all-round self-improvement, just because they can run faster, jump further or hit harder than other people? It should not be necessary for someone to lose so that another may win – not in life, at least.

Being successful does not imply that you have of necessity to be competitive. There is nothing wrong with a bit of healthy competition, taken in good heart and for fun, but striving always to be No. 1 is tantamount to putting everyone else last, and that cannot be what life is all about. Personal success has got to be an enhancement to and an enrichment of personality. Remember your uniqueness! If you can totally accept that, there really is no need to compete with others. Competition is rather like making comparisons – pointing out that one person is 'better' than another. There is no need to compare oneself with others since, in this attitude, lies the seed of envy. By all means take other people as an example to emulate if you see them as having achieved something special and worthy of imitation – but, if you can truly believe in your own uniqueness, it is better to build on that and develop that special sense of self-esteem that will allow you to believe that all things are possible without making comparisons with others.

You would be hard put to find any dictionary definition of success that made any mention of beating others. Winning and losing are merely manifestations of the degree of ability one individual or group (team) has, related to one specific accomplishment, over another individual or group. So, the truth is that success is not a matter of comparing oneself with other people so much as *comparing oneself with oneself* – with one's own capabilities and past achievements. In other words success is an internal happening, not an external one. It is something that requires work and attention all the time. It is persuading our subconscious that we are lovable people capable of great things through our uniqueness and high degree of self esteem.

11. THE IMPORTANCE OF SUCCESS

If your idea of success is beating others, you are certainly starting your journey on the wrong foot.

Success means different things to different people and the truly successful person always knows just what it means to them. One thing that successful people have in common is behaving as if it was impossible to fail. They see themselves as successful and use the power of imaging or positive thinking to sustain this vital self image.

There is little point in aiming to be sucessful in just one area of one's life. Success surely is not simply achieving something of worth but rather becoming a better person in every way as a result of one's actions. Understand that you are greater than anything that can happen to you. If the whole of one's life is enriched as the outcome of the sustained effort required to achieve a particular goal, surely that is achievement of a high order. To become a more rounded, more complete person should be the ultimate aim of anyone interested in self-improvement.

As someone once wisely pointed out, success has many fathers – failure is an orphan. Success is certainly a complicated compound of many ingredients. There is no mystique about it; it is scientifically definable as the knowledge that separates the achievers from the rest – I was tempted to say 'the winners from the losers' but, as I discussed in the previous chapter, that would be strictly incorrect. To be a 'loser' implies that one has striven and failed – and failure is far from being the same thing as non-achievement which is most likely to be the result of indolence, disinterest or simply a lack of suitable motivation.

Sufficient is known about the mechanics of success today to make it predictable. Its predictability, expressed in the most blatantly simplistic terms, comes down to knowing what one must do – AND THEN DOING IT!

Some years ago in the USA there was an investigation into the reasons for the tremendous turn-over of people in the life assurance industry. Two thousand people who had left the industry were sent a comprehensive questionnaire and the eventual evaluation of the vast amount of information that was collated came up with one simple answer – the answer given for their 'failure' by over 80% of all those questioned, 'Nobody told me what to do.' The head of training for a large insurance company in this country told me the reason that, in his experience, so many people fail is that 'they simply don't do what they have been *told* to do.'

How many truly successful people do you know? We have been brainwashed into perceiving public figures, politicians, entertainers, sportsmen, so-called TV personalities, as successful people. Very often their success, if success it be, lies in only one area of their lives – the area for which they have become known to the general public. Many such people only excel because they are doing the only thing they know and understand. They are obsessive about their occupation or skill as a means of achieving fame and fortune.

It is not unknown for sports superstars to be encouraged to develop a 'killer instinct'. Their emotions become excessive and quite unrelated to reality – the task has become obsessive and obliterated many normal human values and attitudes. They become so exposed to the values they are set, or set for themselves, that losing actually becomes a very painful experience. A well-known international tennis star, at his performance peak, was a prime example of the ultimate in positive mental attitude but, being an emotional person, the exaggerated height of mental preparation was probably what caused his famous explosions in the public arena. After these occasions, having been blown apart by the experience, he was apparently overcome by remorse.

We have all heard of the comedian who, offstage, is a tragic figure, sad, morose, disgruntled. Or the millionaire who enjoys little of life and is, all too often, ready and willing to take advantage of other people simply to gain some small, unneeded financial advantage. Yet people will often tell us, having met some well-known personality, that *he was so nice, so genuine*. Could it be that we do not expect famous and successful people to possess those attributes? 'His success hasn't spoilt him a bit!', they cry delightedly. Why on earth should it 'spoil' him? It should be the thing that improved him if it did anything! I suspect our unconscious perception of success is based on the win-lose philosophy and the person who simply enjoys beating or defeating others has little chance of understanding what the real and lasting values really are. True success brings added value to all areas of life and has the ability to not just touch, but actually enrich the lives of others.

The truly successful person is in a privileged position. He can afford to look about him, observe the beneficial effect he can have, if he chooses, on the lives of others. He has no need to take advantage of any other person but can, if he so desired, share his knowledge or wealth with others or make spontaneous gestures of generosity without need of recognition. What a truly enviable state . . .

'The mind is its own place, and in it self
Can make a Heav'n of Hell, a Hell of Heav'n.'
– Milton

12. THE LOOK OF SUCCESS

Naturally successful people are bristling with observable assets:

They are keen and anxious to learn.
They will listen and show a willingness to acquire knowledge.
They ask questions and require comprehensive answers.
They are thinking people and show active curiosity.
They are genuinely interested in others and always willing to help those less fortunate than themselves.
They understand the importance of setting goals and therefore achieve them.
They are people from whom you can 'strike sparks'.
They are not afraid of displaying genuine emotion.
They have a quick and ready empathy and have a great enthusiasm.
They are very positive in their approach to life.
Their lives are not bounded by IF but by WHEN.
They prefer to have everybody win, rather than the 'win-lose' situation.

Life strikes no bargains and makes no promises, no guarantees. All one can do is one's very best but – and this is most important – with expectation.

It is no use going through life 'wishing' and grumbling that you haven't had the breaks – not been given the chances that others have. Success comes through expectation – knowing that you have certain capabilities and also knowing that you have it in your power to be successful. You get what you expect to get out of life, not what you want. The person who cannot see any reason why they should not be able to accomplish something has the greatest chance of real achievement. The creative ability of a child, as we have already seen, is a completely natural thing, based entirely on expectation. A child doesn't sit back and wonder how to do something, it simply gets down to it and does it in a completely natural and uninhibited way. The confusion arises when adults presume to tell the child how things should be done, because the outcome will certainly not be the child's way.

Success does not in any way rely on intelligence or a higher education, but it does have everything to do with belief. With belief, as I have already suggested, anything is possible. Henry Ford said, 'If you believe you can do a thing, or if you believe you cannot – you are right.'

We can just as easily create barriers as remove them. We are capable of placing every stumbling block in our own path, of holding ourselves back and restricting our own potential in so many ways. But not if we have acquired the habit of belief for it is belief that allows us to see the way forward, demolish all barriers and break down restrictions, permitting us to travel to the farthest and most exciting areas of life.

The witch doctor in a primitive tribe has complete sway over his people, even to holding power over life and death. Their belief in his powers is so total that should he tell someone they are going to die, they surely will. In so many forms of medicine, belief is of paramount importance and contributes more to the curative process than the practitioner or his applied treatment. The psychology of the placebo – a harmless medication given to a patient, usually under controlled test conditions – is that a cure may often be effected simply through the patient's belief that medication was administered.

Belief, hope and expectation are strongly linked. We are very much the masters of our destiny so far as expectations go. What you expect to get, you inevitably get. Not what you want – what you *expect*! Expectations concerning the outcome of particular events become our own self-fulfilling prophesies. Going back to healing and the process of recovery from illness, an attitude of hopelessness is a most dangerous situation. The image of 'no recovery' can actually kill, such is the power of the mind.

So, expect good things in life! Good things will surely abound. If you expect bad things – hey presto! bad things! The power of positive thinking!

The expectations – both positive and negative – a parent may have for its child can have a positive bearing on that child's development and attitudes in later life. If parental attitudes were over critical and displayed dissatisfaction, the resultant adult would probably have a tendency to hold back – an attitude reflecting a lack of belief in his or her own ability. Conversely, the positive, loving, supportive parent with a healthy expectation of their child's ability will foster a natural success. Freud made the interesting observation that great men often had doting mothers and it was this adulation that created the confidence to do great things. So, how much controlling power does your past still exert?

Once you can understand and rationalize this you can begin the process of improving and developing a self image that will no longer inhibit your natural progress towards a more successful you.

Human beings have an instinctive craving for success – it is as natural as the wish to remain alive. Everyone has the potential to achieve anything they want . . . but so few people perceive themselves as being successful or indeed feel they have achieved any real success so far in life. Why should this be? There is really no simple answer other than to speculate on the thought that so many people look for outward signs of success whilst, as we have seen, it is an inward manifestation – you must learn to keep the control centre inside you and not allow yourself to be influenced by outside agencies. We will explore this idea further in chapter 15.

Does success have anything to do with ability? Ability is useful, naturally, as is any acquired skill, but, as Napoleon said, 'Ability is of little account without opportunity.'

Success is certainly an inward feeling, but it can also

have an outward look. It does of course have something to do with the particular field of endeavour in which a person may have excelled or experienced particular achievement, but it is unusual to find a truly successful person who is downright scruffy! I am aware that that sounds like an amazingly sweeping statement and it deserves to be contradicted – but it isn't often, I would suggest. Success brings with it a certain pride which usually extends to outward appearances. People will accept you as you present yourself to them. The person who looks successful will be accepted as being successful. This is a brutally superficial assessment but does have a certain relevance to what we are discussing. It has been said often enought that 'you only have one chance to make a first impression.' Who could argue with that as a truism?

It has been observed that in an election of almost any sort, the better looking candidate commands more votes; better looking job applicants are paid more attention and, in life in general, people who are better turned out tend to be noticed more than the scruffier of their peers.

Presenting yourself as a well-packaged proposition may sound a little superficial and unnecessary but it can have considerable relevance, particularly in the context of interviews, meetings and any 'professional' occasions. The sweeping away of class barriers has had a lot to answer for; people cannot easily be identified or categorized by dress these days, so very confusing signals can result. There has been a lot of nonsense spoken and written about dress from a psychological standpoint but there are basic principles that have relevance. Dark suits, for example, are said to create a greater feeling of respect and are seen as being more dignified and authoritive than light ones.

If you dress like a slob, soon you begin to think like a slob – and before long you will act like a slob!

I would not dare to presume to comment on women's dress, other than to say that they tend to have a better sense of occasion and all that is suitable to it, than their male counterparts . . .

Positive action:
1. What sort of a self-image do you have?
   Look at yourself very critically and write down how you feel others would describe you.
2. Now write down how you would describe yourself. How well do the two desriptions coincide?
3. Consider what you think are your best attributes. Consider what you feel are your least attractive features.
4. Now write out another description – *how you would LIKE to be able to describe yourself.*

13. MOTIVATION THROUGH EXPECTATION

In the great world of work, in any large organization, attitudes spread downwards through the pyramidical structure.

A positive boss, full of expectation as to the ability of his employees will have a successful, high performance work-force. He is a boss for whom people will enjoy working. He understands the need for the people below him to set their own goals – possibly sometimes under his direction. At the same time – and I must stress this point – it is very important that individuals are allowed, even encouraged whenever possible to set their own goals. If goals are set solely by a superior, the employee simply becomes an automaton, submissively fulfilling someone else's requirements. It does nothing for their personal motivation or self-esteem to feel that a superior is unwilling to allow them to set goals for themselves – and the inevitable outcome will be resentment. Remember that all important spring-board to achievement – desire? – that is the ingredient that is likely to be missing when goals are set by a superior.

Performance will always be at its lowest under the

dogmatic, critical and condemnatory boss, for whom the work force feel, at best, total indifference.

A prime example of the reality of right attitudes in action was to be seen in the first company I worked for which, when I joined it, was still very new. It was a company positively enthused with the excitement of expectation. Throughout the entire administration and sales force there was such a positive anticipation of and belief in accomplishment that the operation could scarcely have been anything but the huge success it was. Right from day one they had a system in operation at every level by which each individual had to produce a report on the person immediately below him or her every month. Everyone was naturally aware of this and the practice generated such energy that the electricity positively flooded through the corporate structure in both directions, upwards and outwards.

At that point in the company's development, there was a strong corporate enthusiasm. The question was not just how things should be done, but why. There was a sensitively questioning approach to problem solving – an unusual display of corporate understanding demonstrating awareness for the supreme importance of attitude when dealing with human beings. The senior management knew and recognized that corporate success depended on people, and, understanding that fundamental principle, were quick to establish themselves as a company that people wanted to work for.

The good boss is always aware of the value of

recognition – that pat-on-the-back everyone needs from time to time. It not only shows an awareness of what each individual is doing but it also expresses thanks for what has been achieved. Finally, it enhances the feelings of expectation and belief in the person's ability. These may appear small and trivial things, and probably that is the reason they are so easily and so often neglected, even forgotten, yet they are vitally important to human relationships. To maintain authority does not imply any disregard for human values, though, sadly, this is an attitude seen all too often. Discipline, coupled with mutual respect is not such a difficult balance to achieve. One very simple rule with great relevance is praise publicly, reprimand privately. Another is to understand the difference between capabilities and effectiveness. The real achievers are not the people who simply work to their capabilities but the ones among us who combine effectiveness and ability to sell their ideas to those around them.

To maintain a high motivational level, the flow of goodwill must operate in both directions.

Although reward and recognition flow downwards through the organization, it is not unusual that ideas and concepts are developed at the lower end of the scale and are passed upwards. Woe to the employer who disregards this or cannot see the benefit of allowing that good ideas can emanate from other sources than himself. The boss may have a reasonably clear vision in broad brush terms of the whole corporate scene but it is at the lower end of the corporate structure where detail – the fine brush strokes to the picture – can often be added to greatest effect and with real and lasting value. Nothing is more dispiriting to the employee than having his ideas or suggestions swept aside, or, worst of all, totally ignored.

It is not unknown for a salaried boss to resent the idea that a commission-earning salesman may be making more money than he earns himself. Could there be anything more ridiculous? Any employer should be delighted – and be prepared and willing to show it – if every one of his salespeople earns more than he does! Such a situation can only mean that his is a very well motivated organization – and, if that is the case, the results obviously will be reflected in his own earnings.

One of the greatest lessons we can learn from life is that the way we *think* and the way we *are* can have the most profound effect on those around us.

Positive action:
1. If you are an employer, are you getting the best from your staff? Do you ever reward them over and above your obligations?
2. Do you lead by beckoning or pointing? Consider this carefully. Is there room for any beneficial adjustment?
3. Ask yourself whether you are able to accept suggestions and ideas from your employees. How much value do you place on such things?
4. Write down what you believe your employees think of you. Is your answer anywhere near the way in which you would like to be thought of? Do you feel there are beneficial adjustments that could be made?

14. LEARNING AND THE NEED FOR PROGRAMMING

'Success breeds success' is a saying that, as a child always baffled me! It didn't seem to make sense. The reality of life has shown me what a truth it is though – it relates to what I have come to think of as 'The Human Dynamo'.

Remember the strange energy that attracted people to the studio of the painter? That was a perfect example of 'the human dynamo' in action and revealed it simply as the energy or electricity we are able to generate within ourselves which can act as a magnet, attracting people in harmony with our dominant thinking, towards us.

The energy our minds produce radiates outwards like the beam of a lighthouse and the effects can be felt, even at considerable distances, by others who are in tune with us. Most of us have had the experience of thinking about someone who, seemingly miraculously, has immediately contacted us. There are dangers, as with most things in life, since this power can work in both a positive and a negative way. Negative thoughts will attract negative circumstances and negative people. Never overlook the fact that whatever your dominant thought patterns are at any particular time, they will attract similar feelings towards you.

The process could be described as *resonance*. If you struck a tuning fork in a room containing a violin, the string corresponding to that note would begin to vibrate in sympathy. Resonance.

So, the world around you – your external world – is simply a reflection of your inner state, what is going on in your own mind.

What an amazing power this is! It allows the possibility for changing the world immediately around you by changing the world within you. You have the ability to change and affect relationships to the extent that the way people treat you will be nothing more nor less than a reflection of your own personality and attitudes.

The implications of all this must, by now, be becoming abundantly clear. Perhaps you believe in destiny as a force over which we have little or no control – something which lies beyond the scope of our influence. Only you can decide what you feel about that. However, the one thing you can control is what goes on in your own mind – and through that you do have a definite opportunity to influence the circumstances that surround you. It is the quality of that influence that can and will have such a profound effect on your life.

We cannot literally bring about change to the external world – attempts to do that merely produce unhappiness. What we can do – and it is monumental as a concept – is to alter our own inner world and observe the benefits that it produces upon the world about us. Change the way you are thinking and you will, as a result, change your reality.

The power I am talking about is often described as the power of positive thinking, or Positive Mental Attitude (PMA). Remember though, this is a power not concerned with wanting but with *expecting*!

At this point in your life – as you may realize from what you have read so far – you are the sum total of all you have ever been told, thought or experienced, both positive and negative! Alarming thought, isn't it? If life doesn't seem to you to be all it could be, you can do something about it. The changes have to take place in your own mind, and there is one ingredient that will play the star role in achieving a new mental attitude – BELIEF. It is believing that these things are not only possible but will be brought about.

As we have seen, our minds are machines that operate on two levels. The conscious mind is the part we think and reason with, whilst the second level is that which is controlling our daily activity and dealing with all the mundanities of simply being alive. It is performing millions of functions every second as it activates every movement we make, every action we take. Computer-like, it never ceases translating every thought, sight, sound and sensation into action through the process of comparative assessment and the resultant feedback.

It is miraculous that we are able to drive a car whilst listening to music and thinking about our everyday problems. Often we arrive at a destination without remembering much about the journey, the situations we negotiated, the actions we took, and yet we arrived safely! Consider the mental processes that went on during that journey: the computations of speed, distance, breaking power, time, happened spontaneously, continuously, with action after action being taken whilst another part of the brain responded to music and rambled amongst the problems of the day. The actions required and the messages sent and received that made that journey possible were activated at the subconscious level of our brain – that 'bio-computer' that is forever comparing past and present experiences – producing what we think of as automatic actions. This is not the rational, reasoning part of the brain but the part that only reacts to *instructional programming*. You may marvel at the computer on your desk yet, as likely as not, you take for granted how much more miraculous your own brain is.

Many people have gone through life so far literally causing their own failure simply because they have been programmed by restrictive attitudes right from the start. Clearly, if you agree that a better set of circumstances should prevail, your job now is to unscramble the muddle and begin re-programming to become the person you expect to be.

Staying with the computer analogy, properly prepared programming instructions must be produced to ensure that the machine can perform the tasks expected of it. These instructions are fed into the computer's memory so that every action it takes is the result of planned commands. At the subconscious level the human mind works in much the same way – it is not, just as a computer is not, a thinking mechanism. It is a mechanism that responds to commands based on the information provided. It is incapable of being either logical or critical. The more precise the information, the better and more effective will be the outcome. Such a process is what we have come to call learning . . .

Programming entails emptying out the unwanted commands that produce conditioned response, and re-programming with new commands – commands that will help to develop the instinctive habit of success. Army training is a splendid example of programming – achieved through endless rehearsal (training) – to produce instant, unquestioning response. A lot of the learning process is no more than rehearsal – for rehearsing a situation is a sure means of bringing about a desired result.

Positive action:
1. Get into the habit of 'rehearsing' events and their outcome. Before an interview, decide on what you want the outcome to be and rehearse it over and over in your mind, trying to visualize exactly how the conclusion will arrive.
2. If you are a salesman or woman, rehearse the discussion you expect to have with your prospective customer and visualize its outcome. See yourself as successful. Imagine how you will feel as you walk away from each successful sale. And imagine how pleased your customer will feel at the purchase he or she has just made.
3. Get into the habit of visualization and get to know just what success *feels* like.

15. CONDITIONING FOR SUCCESS

Right at the outset of this book I suggested you get rid of everything in your life that is of no benefit of use – including old clothes! In other words, to rid yourself of all accumulated ballast that is an unnecessary burden.

DID YOU DO IT?

The suggestion was intended as a preliminary exercise – something to make you feel good, and something to help put you in a receptive frame of mind before you delved too far into the book. But I wonder if you did it . . .

We are now back to clearing out time again! The moment has arrived when we should start clearing out the dusty recesses of the mind – and the very first thing we are faced with is getting rid of, once and for all, the 'could do better' label. You have always been able to do better! Let's accept that as a fact – why else would you be reading this? So, we are now laying down the procedures and ground rules to make sure that **best** becomes the permanent state.

Do you feel that you are a unique individual?

Consider this – out of the entire population of the world, you could be identified beyond any doubt by finger prints, blood group, voice print and quite a few other means of pin-pointing a specific human being with both precision and exactitude. That, surely, must make you totally unique?

But those are merely scientific ways of cataloguing you. To be unique because of a series of features over which you have no possible control is no real claim to individuality! Fingerprints and all the other para-phernalia of identification are merely the 'name and address' on the package – this shell within which we live is just the vehicle that we conveniently use to carry around the really unique bits of ourselves – *the mind* and the soul.

Do you feel that you are in control of your own life?

or

Do you feel that external circumstances dominate you?
Are you over-shadowed by your debts, your job,
your boss, your health?

If this is the case, then things have got a little out of proportion and the evidence suggests that the centre of your control lies, as it were, outside your body. This is a state which allows no scope for flexibility, creativity or any potential for beneficial development.

It is our thoughts and expectations that are most likely to affect our actions so, clearly, the power centre of control must be on the inside. If external elements are controlling you then life can only be dull, worrisome and mundane. The successful person – the high achiever – is a far happier, far more balanced and self-fulfilled person because he has kept the control centre within himself.

And what about your emotions? Are you happy, sad, excited, fearful? Your behaviour at any specific point in time will be governed by your thought patterns. Do you agree with that statement?

Your actions then, are the result of thoughts. Is it not logical to suggest that, if you are in control of your thoughts, you are in control of your actions and therefore are determining the way your life is shaping and moving? By the same token, if you are not in control of your thoughts – implying that the control is on the outside – your actions will be unpredictible, unplanned and utterly haphazard. That process can never lead to any kind of satisfactory fulfilment or self-improvement.

Remember that you become what you think, so it is important to do everything you can to get your thinking right! What is thinking but *planning*?

We spend most of our time talking to ourselves – the constant discourse between our conscious and subconscious – and, as we know, our subconscious will accept whatever we say either as a truth, or as an instruction or command. It is of supreme importance that we make only positive statements – and never make any declaration about ourselves that we would not wish to become reality. Try also never to make negative or destructive statements. There is a kind of negative chemistry that occurs in the body as a result of negative thoughts which can attract the very things to you that you fear or dislike most. 'I' – as in 'I can't', 'I am tired', 'I will try' etc – is the trigger to make your subconscious sit up and really take notice. It is taken as the signal that precedes a command so that whatever follows will be recorded in that form.

I have already mentioned the influence and effect that parents and teachers can have on children and how, as a result of programmed attitudes, certain behavioural patterns have been carried into adult life. Many of these influencs will have been good, others may have left feelings of hurt which may have become very difficult to forgive. If this is your own experience, the time has come to redress the balance.

To clear out the effects of these attitudes from our adult life and to allow us to become whole, fully-functioning grown-ups we must develop a conscious attitude of forgiveness. Let any blame you may have been harbouring go completely. If you feel it will achieve the desired end, say out loud 'I completely forgive so-and-so'. Drop any form of grudge or disappointment you may have felt towards anyone who could have influenced you and forgive them completely – then enjoy the good feelings that will come to you by doing this.

This simple act doesn't really have much to do with the other person – indeed, they are probably totally unaware of any of the feelings you may have been unconsciously harbouring.

It is an action concerned with very personal and

possibly very deep-seated emotions. It is carried out to enhance and enrich your own peace of mind and can also have a profound effect in the process of change we are aiming to achieve.

Do you feel that *you* are possibly to blame for some of the attitudes you have – and, indeed, for what you have become? Then forgive yourself too! – for all your foolish deeds, all the indiscretions and follies you have perpetrated – forgive yourself totally and then – FORGET IT!

In attempting to straighten our our thinking we are dealing with two polarities – *desire and fear*.

Desires are not the same as wishes which, as we know, are usually only hazy hopes, loosely directed toward some inaccurately defined ideal. Desires are the solid fuel of achievement and little can be brought about without real desire as a starting point. The stronger the desire, coupled with a total belief that achievement is possible, the more certain will be the outcome.

The real key to change, then, is to keep your mind on your desires and keep it off your fears. Fears are the deeply buried and 'forgotten' legacies of upbringing – the triggers that activate conditioned responses. Fears are the things that can make us feel unaccountably unhappy, whilst desires stimulate us.

It seems to me – and I am in no way a qualified psychologist – that to simply try to repress unwanted feelings is doing no more than making sure we retain them by pushing them deeper into our subconscious –

and anything that remains there always has the potential to re-surface in the future.

These negative feelings, then, must become completely overshadowed by much stronger emotions so that positive attitudes emerge before fear can get out of its front door – as Franklin D. Roosevelt said, 'the only thing we have to fear is fear itself'. So how do we set about combating fear? Fear of any sort is a negative influence of the worst kind and so the weapon we use must be so positive as be able to overcome it totally – and that weapon is your own desire to succeed!

Let your mind become so obsessed with what you expect and with the feelings you know you will experience through achievement that there will be little time for it to dwell on unimportant fears and worries. It is solutions at which we are aiming all our thoughts, not gearing them to problems.

Laying plans is vital. Both our successes and our failures are the outcome of our thoughts. Has it ever occurred to you that people who fail do actually PLAN their own downfall? Not intentionally, of course, but simply by having negative thought patterns. Expecting to fail is a sure way to ensure that you do!

Unsuccessful people share one factor that distinguishes them – they know all the reasons for failure. They know all the alibis that will explain away their own lack of achievement.

Alibis are no more than excuses –

'If only I had more time . . .'
'If only I wasn't so tired . . .'

Don't play the 'if only' game – and don't indulge in building alibis. As you must know by now, you are simply playing into the hands of that subconscious of yours yet again – the mechanism that, used intelligently, will always be your greatest ally.

The Human Dynamo will draw people and circumstances to you, but it is just as capable of doing precisely the opposite by running in reverse. As with a magnet, there is a positive and negative aspect, as we have seen, and it is just as easy to repel circumstances or people as it is to attract them – but only if your thinking it at fault.

Too many people, although not exactly unsuccessful, rely on accident or chance to bring results. They label it luck – although it is extraordinary how one's 'luck' increases in a direct ratio to the amount of energy one is creating through sheer hard work and right thinking!

'All I need is a bit of luck', 'being in the right place at the right time', 'the luck of the draw', 'not what you know, but who you know' . . . all these often heard remarks are simply evidence of reliance on outside circumstances rather than creating the right sort of thought patterns that will *influence* outside circumstances.

If you want to rely on luck, that's entirely up to you – but remember, you are playing the long odds. Plan effectively, work harder at success-producing projects, and, absolutely no doubt about it, you will shorten the odds significantly – and your 'luck' will increase! Remember? – success breeds success . . .

Recognition of opportunity is one of the natural outcomes of right thinking. But what is opportunity? There are many people who wouldn't spot an opportunity if it jumped up and bit them. Opportunities can offer great scope to the negative thinker! How often have you heard someone declare: 'it's not worth doing that – it's been done before'. Is that the cry of the would-be entrepreneur?

Why do you think around 300 restaurants close down in Britain each year? More significantly, why do you think approximately 300 restaurants open in Britain every year? Human beings are generally amazingly resilient and, at their best, have a splendid capacity for believing in themselves. They do not willingly accept the idea that defeat or failure can touch them, and love to believe that they can succeed where others have failed. It may seem blind, but what a splendid attitude this is! Without it nothing would ever be achieved.

The first law of opportunity is never turn an idea down because it has been tried – and yet, unfortunately, that is exactly what is happening all the time.

At the time of writing, the country – and indeed the world, it would seem – is in a state of recession, creating a climate in which negative thinking could so easily prevail. That is unless a sufficient number of people apply really positive thinking both to their own and to the problems in the wider international spectrum – thoughts and ideas with the capability of inspiring and revitalizing both the individual and the general situation. The media has dwelt far too long on the down-side and is in danger of demotivating our population to a point where all effort might, to the individual, appear futile in a land bereft of opportunity and creative thinking.

There are two negative attitudes embodied in the 'it's been done' syndrome. The first is the implication that it was tried and failed because it wasn't a good idea – not allowing for the possibility that maybe it wasn't done the right way, and that another individual might have approached the opportunity from an entirely different angle which could have made it work! The second is that 'it's been done' therefore there is no point in doing it yourself – again allowing no flexibility of thought or action.

Procrastination is the enemy of achievement.

Living by hope and accident is allowing your life to be controlled and contorted by outside forces and circum-stances, drifting through life like a rudderless ship, never quite seeing things in sharp focus because there has been no attempt to make clear plans and set defined goals. This lack of directional thrust often leads to unhappiness which, in its turn, creates negative thinking. The result of this cycle is a tendency to become even more negative. Frustration increases, boredom, the prince of subversion and indolence, takes over and life is seen as pretty pointless as the slide further down this demotivational spiral continues.

Human beings need to achieve and, even more, need to see their achievement recognized. The perpetual under-achiever is a sad person, but if he only realized it, the solution is in his own hands – or more precisely, his own head. He can free himself from these woolly attitudes which lack direction by taking positive and permanent control of his thoughts and pulling the centre into himself. Remember what the power of positive thinking can do – whatever you concentrate your thoughts on grows and the constant repetition will eventually turn the thought into reality. Success is a state of mind.

The concept of success is relative to age, circumstance and environment. It is different things to different people. To a child it may be acquiring a longed-for bicycle or getting into a school team. To a teenager it may be having a date with some very special person. To an adult it might be surrounding oneself with all the visible status symbols, the trappings of perceived success. To an elderly retired person it might simply be getting to the shops and back in the face of some physical adversity. In each case there are two common denominators – THE SETTING AND ACHIEVEMENT OF GOALS.

Positive action:
1. Do make sure that you have answered all the questions posed in this chapter.
2. Resolve only to involve yourself in success-producing projects.
3. Don't waste time trying to resurrect lost causes or in flogging dead horses. There are always new and positive projects to pursue.

16. PUTTING IT ALL TOGETHER

As we grow older and hopefully more mature, we become more and more self-directed. That is not to say we become any wiser. Also, in our general development, energy levels tend to diminish as we approach our optimum perceived potential. In everyone's working life there is a point at which they peak – very likely this is just before they reach that point I referred to earlier in the book as their *level of incompetence*. As with all peaks, the only way is down – not necessarily willingly, but because it is clear that up is no longer the available option. By the very nature of things these happenings are likely to coincide with what we would loosely call middle age – and the coincidence can go further, for this is the point also where redundancy, if it is a possibility, could so easily occur. The candidate's best years are behind him or her, and even though experience and reliability are valuable assets, these are often the people to suffer redundancy – and to suffer it at a time when it can be a considerable blow. Employers like using terms such as 'natural wastage' and 'early retirement' to make themselves feel less like the villain of the piece.

These are the circumstances – and more so if they coincide with middle age – when it is difficult to define or find acceptable goals. A person without goals is a person without a sense of direction and the outcome is a feeling of utter hopelessness.

This may well have been your own experience – or at least the experience of someone you know. So, having read this far you have, I sincerely hope, picked yourself up, dusted yourself down and are ready and eager to start all over again!

Goal setting can have many beneficial effects. The state of inertia and hopelessness disappears with the achievement of a sense of direction. Goals trigger behavioural patterns and their consequences maintain them, so goal-setting is the start of an important building process. By degrees self-confidence will return, amplified by desire and belief. Motivation begins to appear and the ability to solve problems and to think clearly is boosted. Expectation of achievement is a wonderfully uplifting feeling.

Everyone is a potential success! It is just that, for one reason or another, and on a purely temporary basis, some of us are disguised as failures! – the fault of the unexpected or simply of past influences. Our immediate task, then, is to produce our 'programme' in the form of goals and expectations. There must be nothing sloppy or haphazard about this.

Everyone, at some time or other, has indulged in dreaming of the things they would like to possess, or the things they would like to achieve, and the places they would like to visit. Unfortunately – for we are looking here at a rather negative self-indulgence –

116

sometimes, these 'dreams' are rooted in envy of the achievements and possessions of other people. 'Wishes' can sometimes be based on doubts, probably unconscious; we are not really believing that the attainment of such things is possible for us, so resort to wishing such things might begin to come our way.

Wishing, as we now know, is little more than hoping – and 'hope' is simply clinging to the vagueness of possibility.

So, considering these factors, how likely is it that our dreams will become reality? The likelihood is somewhat remote . . . unless we can formulate an approach that allows all things to be come possible. Three key words are missing from the pattern we have just considered, and the missing words are already very familiar to us. They are, of course, *desire, belief and expectation*.

Anything the human mind can conceive and believe in is achievable.

Whoever it was that originally made that profound statement really understood the secret of success.

All attempts at change or betterment must start with desire and expectation, and it must be desire of a very high order. For example, to give up the habit of smoking is not as difficult as most people like to think. They tend to make silly noises about the idea because they know they *should* give up, but quite simply, *they have no **desire** to give up*.

So, returning to the theme of dreams, let's replace

'wishing' with 'desire' and then 'hope' with 'belief'. The entire imagery of the 'dreaming' process has now changed – in fact, it is dreaming no longer. The concept has been altered in a way that will allow all things to be achievable!

Consider the 'staircase' of achievement that follows – it shows the degrees of expression related to the desire to achieve goals as it moves from a state of total negativism of 'I will not' to the ultimate success of 'I did!'

100% – I did!
90% – I will
80% – I can
70% – I think I can
60% – I might
50% – I think I might
40% – Could I?
30% – I wish I could
20% – I don't know how
10% – I can't
0% – I won't

Because you are reading this book you are obviously interested in change, but – and I hope you will now agree as I cannot emphasize this point too strongly – it is no use whatsoever simply wishing for change to come about. All the desired changes must be pinned down precisely and in writing, set out clearly as a collection of goals.

The subconscious has no sense of time passing and

does not reason – it simply acts on what it knows to be 'true' – and truth, in this context, means *what it has been told*.

Some motivational writers will advocate that goals should be expressed in writing as though they had already been achieved. I have my doubts about the advisability of this because, in dealing with the subconscious, we must always remember it is not a reasoning machine. It could be misled by statements that suggest the goal has already been achieved.

Make your goals ambitious, stretching, yet realizable, and express them in as much detail as possible. The better the directions and instructions, the more likely it is that the amazing mechanism within you will be awakened and show itself able to act on the requirements.

A time-scale is important. All goals should be pinned down by a point of arrival – the achievement. You have probably heard of 'Parkinson's Law', one aspect of which states that any task will take up the amount of time allotted to it. Your subconscious is not concerned with time so can be expected to work within any time-scale it is given, always providing that you are being realistic.

In setting goals it is not your concern to know *how* they are to be achieved. Your subconscious will dictate that, always providing your desires and beliefs are sufficiently strong.

★

A PERSONAL NOTE TO MY READER . . .

I would not be in the least surprised if, at this point, you are beginning to experience a sneaky scepticism! Why not? If you have not encountered ideas of this calibre before, scepticism is a perfectly understandable reaction.

I hope very much that, having read this far, you will have an idea of the potential that lies within each and every one of us. The ideas I am putting to you are as much to awaken your consciousness to enable you to start a process of regeneration as to provide you with precise instructions. Attempts at any sort of change represent a most exciting journey and, as with any journey, the unexpected can always occur. I can only hold your hand through the early stages of your own personal exploration. You will discover routes of your own by chance.

What I am proposing is not some fanciful concept of my own, it is a truth known by many but experienced by far too few. What I would ask you to try and do is put aside your doubts and try to totally accept the ideas I am offering you. The most powerful thing you have at your disposal is, in the first place your desire to bring about change or achieve a particular goal, and, in the second place, sufficient belief to carry it through.

One further word to the sceptic – in establishing and writing down your list of goals, if you were one of those unfortunate people hit by redundancy, job-loss or business collapse and you felt you had lost everything, you have absolutely nothing more to lose by trying anything that might put you back in control of your own life!

There is a technique commonly used on people suffering from acute depression. It is based on the idea that modesty is bad for your brain as it can cause you to fail to recognize your own strengths – and thus become increasingly pessimistic. The patient is encouraged to write down a list of things they are good at, in the form 'I am observant', 'I am intelligent' etc. and told to repeat the list to themselves several times a day, rewarding themselves with some small treat at the end. Their happiness increases and, and it does so, the brain becomes more alert.

The process of building up your self-esteem is of paramount importance to the process of change and development. Please, do not deny yourself the possibility of entering a new world of affluence and contentment. What can you possibly lose other than a little time? – and you probably have too much of that anyway!

Give it your very best shot – really go for it! A drowning man doesn't reject the hand stretched out to him on the grounds that he hasn't been introduced!

One other important point to remember, right at the outset of this exercise. Keep what you are doing, or about to do, very much to yourself – for the time being, at least. You are just as frail and vulnerable as the next person when it comes to being undermined by somebody else's scepticism!

I hope you feel that you have already discovered quite a lot about yourself and the way in which your mind functions. It would be all too easy at this stage to allow a partner or friend to ridicule what you are attempting, producing their own brand of negativism simply because they haven't had the benefit of all the explanation and preparation that has lead us to this point in our exploration of the possible.

A healthy scepticism then is perfectly acceptable and understandable – but don't let it be your excuse to do nothing – remember what inertia can do! You bought this book! – at least that shows that you are open to suggestion and anxious to investigate the possibility of change and to benefit from all the opportunities it can bring.

★

Let's summarize our journey so far . . .

We have talked a great deal already about belief as the all-important attitude when considering success and achievement.

The human mind, by the most simplistic and basic of layman's definitions, is divided into two parts. The conscious function is what we use ceaselessly as we live our daily lives and communicate both with others – through speech, sight, hearing, touch – and with ourselves – through thinking. The thought process is concerned far more with language than with visual images. The visual does, of course, come into the process, but the pictures are accompanied by a constant 'voice over'. In the recognition function, think what is happening when we tap someone on the shoulder, in the belief that we know them, but the moment they turn around, we recognize our mistake – it is only someone who looks a little – and probably very superficially – like the person for whom we mistook them.

Our apology is instant! – but think of the miraculous process that has just taken place. Messages involving both words and pictures have been flashed to the subconscious 'computer' where they have been passed to the amazing memory bank of total past experience. They have been subjected to a process of sorting, evaluation and comparison to provide the feed-back that tells us we have made a mistake. And the whole process took milli-seconds.

The subconscious, as we have seen, is, like the computer, programmable. Take, as a simple example, the act of walking. It is not necessary for us to 'think' how to walk. We would say this is because we 'know' how to achieve it. We did, however, have to learn the process through hard experience and constant practice – until all the information required to accomplish this amazingly complex operation was safely stored, available for instant recall.

And so it is with every single movement we make. When we encounter a new task, new programming is required. If the task involves repetition, as with, say, a production line process, performance improves as familiarity with the task increases. Rehearsal and constant repetition produce better and more efficient performance as the flow of information and the resultant feed-back pass to and from the subconscious, constantly subjecting the process to adjustment, honing and perfecting.

Is it possible for the subconscious to make mistakes – for the process to break down? Recently I saw an amazing piece of film in which a member of an Olympic diving team appeared to go completely out of control, tumbling through the air to hit the water in a most painful and untidy way. The acrobatic performance that was intended would have been the result of endless practice and programming until something as near perfection as possible was achieved. Why then did it 'go wrong'? It was the diver's concentration and mental preparation that faltered at the critical moment when the programme should have taken over. The reason, most likely, was nervousness or perhaps the contestant was distracted in some way just at the crucial moment.

Why do we use the expression 'I'd like to sleep on it' when we are confronted by the need for the answer to a difficult problem?

Instinctively, it would seem, we are all aware that 'something happens' during the process of sleep which is vaguely to do with the solving of problems – *and yet so few people actually put this wonderful capacity to any real or intentional use*.

So, the subconscious is capable of solving problems, and by doing so, provides indicators that will aid you in taking the correct action in relation to your original question. This is why – and I must repeat this – it is not for you to worry over *how* something is to come about. The instructions will be provided. Don't be impatient. These answers are not necessarily going to appear immediately. But, be sure of one thing – they *will* appear. It is up to you to be alert and ready to receive the information which might come as a mere passing thought or a sudden hunch.

Your subconscious then, is a most remarkable piece of equipment, grossly under-used as a tool to aid you in achieving desired goals. Think of the resource you have at your disposal! Through deliberate programming, your subconscious can aid you in so many ways. Most of the things we do in our day to day lives are what we refer to as 'automatic'. They are habits, but like the walking process, had to be learned, practised and perfected. The information was then stored away to be recalled at any time to repeat the action without 'thinking'.

Can you accept the idea, then, that success could become a habit?

As with everything you have ever learned to do, **it is possible to learn to be successful**. The key to achieving this is simply your own total belief in the fact that it *is* possible. It then becomes a case of creating a set of programming instructions as the basis for what the subconscious is expected to do . . .

Positive action . . . is now the keynote for the rest of the book, so, go to it – and enjoy what it will bring . . .

17. ACQUIRING THE HABIT OF SUCCESS

Everything you do must be carried out with total belief. That is, not just belief in your ability to achieve the goals you have set yourself, but belief in yourself as the person you expect to be, and belief in the attainment of the items you will shortly be asked to list, both abstract and physical.

The instructions to be fed to your subconscious must be both credible and acceptable – and obviously it is important that you are able to believe in their accomplishment.

The instructions we are about to produce for our programming are declarations of one sort or another. When we are considering character changes and the modification of personal habits, all the declarations must be presented in the present tense, i.e. as though they had already taken place. The building of self-image is a continuous process and it is important that you perceive yourself in a perpetual state of change, development and improvement.

Declarations aimed at material advantages such as the acquisition of a particular car, should be expressed in the future tense, as expectations. There are subtle differences in these two approaches. Some people will tell you that *all* declarations should be expressed in the present tense, as that is a very powerful state in terms of visualization. I tend to the idea that, with all we know about the subconscious, the present tense is a confusing state when it comes to material declarations. You either have the car you want or you don't! There are no degrees of possession. To tell your subconscious that you have a particular car as a means of acquiring it does not make sense.

There is, in effect, nothing to do, no action to take – it has apparently been taken and the result achieved!

The fine-tuning of character and behavioural patterns, being a slow but constantly fluid process, leaves constant scope for the subconscious through its perpetual function of assessment and evaluation.

In both the initial writing out of declarations, and in the subsequent use of them, it is important to try and visualize just how you will feel at the attainment of any of your goals. This is all part of your belief. Suppose you have a real desire to lose weight. You must be able to imagine yourself thinner and enjoy the sensation of greater mobility, better health, a personal image that is very attractive both to you and to other people. The closer you can get to experiencing the *reality* of the outcome the better.

Do remember that *HOW* your goals are to be achieved is the job of the subconscious. If you start making it your concern and worrying about it you are simply starting a process of self-doubt – and *there is absolutely no room for attitudes of that sort in the process we are about to set in motion.* You will eventually be provided with all the directional pointers that will show you what your next step should be.

Let's make a start by taking a searching look at you, the person we are hoping to modify . . .

Begin – right now. Start by taking out a blank sheet of paper and writing down what you see as all your positive aspects. Write these attributes down in the present tense . . .

I am a dynamic person . . .
I am forceful and persuasive . . .
I have an excellent and very retentive memory . . .
I am popular, likeable and make friends easily . . .
I am physically attractive to others
etc. etc.

Make your list in the form of a series of definite statements. Take time over this and include literally everything you can think of. This is a list of things to do with your own self-image and self-esteem. Include not only what you believe to be your best points, but everything you would like to think others think is true of you.

(PLEASE DO NOT READ BEYOND THIS
PAGE UNTIL YOUR LIST IS COMPLETED
TO YOUR ENTIRE SATISFACTION)

When you have completed that list . . .

. . . begin another on the basis of what you see as all your negative traits (those things you feel could be bettered, eliminated, or modified) – again in the form of statements . . .

I am always late for appointments . . .
I smoke too much . . .
I am lazy and put things off when I can
I eat too much
I do not pay my wife and family sufficient attention
etc. etc.

Be thoroughly honest with yourself and don't pull your punches – try to see yourself as others may possibly see you.

(AGAIN, PLEASE COMPLETE THIS TASK BEFORE READING ANY FURTHER)

Between the two lists you have made you should now have a fairly comprehensive catalogue of the positive and negative you!

Do you like what you see?
How honest have you been?
Have you let yourself off lightly – or even perhaps been too harsh in your self criticism?

Consider your lists carefully – take time and really think about it.

Is there anything you should add or would like to retract?

Look at your positive statements – do they represent the 100% situation?

Are you, for example totally forceful and persuasive?
Is your memory perfect?
Don't you have any enemies – or *are* there people who dislike you?

Taking a scale of 0 to 100% put a rating beside every statement you have made – both positive and negative.

So, what sort of a person have you shown yourself to be now? Perfect and without need of improvement? Possibly putting in the percentage ratings has given you yet another perspective on yourself! – one that now allows plenty of scope for attempting at least a modicum of change.

Which negative trait would be the first you would like to change? Your answer might be:

'I am lazy and put things off when I can'

How do we set about putting this to rights? Simply by wishing to be more dynamic? I don't think so! Remember everything we know about our subconscious and about the flimsy concept of 'wishing'? Your subconscious must be told precisely what is expected of it.

So, a new sheet of paper! This time write down something along these lines. . .

I have a great deal of drive and my energy
increases every day.
Because I am successful, I always do things NOW!
I never put off until tomorrow what I can do today
etc. etc.

Declarations of that sort put the concept of laziness and inertia firmly in their places through very positive statements. Continue this process until you have firmly pinned down every negative trait. Again, spend time over this exercise until you feel satisfied that you have a list of positive statements about the YOU you intend to bring into existence – a you with a very clear self-image and, above all, strong self esteem.

I suggest you intersperse your list with a few general statements. Some of the following may be of help.

I like myself – I am a warm, friendly, well-liked person
My thinking is very creative – and my mind
expands every day
I am enthusiastic about everything I undertake
My health is excellent – I feel better and more
energetic every day
I do not waste time on negative thoughts or mix
with negative people
I start work promptly each day and bring vigour
and energy to every task
I know I am capable of achieving everything I
set out to do
I am successful in everything I undertake and enjoy
all the rewards that my success brings
I am always seeking to improve in every aspect of
my life because I know that is the true route to success
I always bring total concentration to any
task I undertake
I am able to relax totally when I need to conserve
my energy
I set my goals high and attain them easily because
I declare and affirm them constantly
I am considerate to other people and always
respect their feelings
I follow up every good idea I have and make the
very most of it
I greatly enjoy meeting people. My relaxed attitude

stimulates their confidence in me and brings
enrichment both to my experience and theirs

What we have so far is a list of statements that are
aimed at adjusting and improving your attitudes. Let's
now add a few more things to the list, but this time
concentrating on the more material aspects such as
income and possessions.

ANOTHER NOTE! – THIS TIME, EXPRESSLY TO MY BRITISH READERS . . .

We the British have a strange attitude towards the
accumulation of wealth and personal possessions!

Happily our past hang-ups are not quite so noticeable
in the 1990s, but many older readers may still suffer
from vague sensations of discomfort when the accumulation of wealth is mentioned – a feeling perhaps that
there is something faintly disgraceful about wanting
riches!

Let's sweep this quaint and misguided notion out of
the way immediately. If you were to become seriously
rich, would it really bother you? I very much doubt it!
I suspect that the reason we pretend to be disinterested
in wealth is because we have subconsciously decided
we are never likely to acquire it – and yet perhaps,
secretly, we envy it in others! Hypocrisy of this sort
has got to go!

In this country too, we tend to have a very strange
view of success and the obvious trappings that may
accompany it. We have been infused with the idea of

work as a noble and worthy undertaking – the work ethic – and yet, the acquiring of wealth as a result of hard work has a stigma attached to it. I suspect this goes back to the Industrial Revolution, the subsequent and necessary formation of workers unions and the whole concept of bosses and workers in a state of fervent and perpetual conflict. The employer's state of affluence was despised and yet the labouring clases accepted that they could never hope to aspire to being anything other than what they were. With thoughts like that they were clearly doomed to the inevitability of their self-image.

Compare this view with 'The American Dream' – the idea that anyone can achieve anything – even to becoming the President of The United States of America! With a clear-minded belief of that calibre, success will always be something worthy of the greatest admiration – never envy – for success is taken to be an example for all to emulate. This is what makes Americans such 'professionals'! Everyone is a professional at whatever he or she does. There is status and a natural dignity that goes with every activity, no matter how humble, and this is what stimulates the attitude of total professionalism and pride in achievement.

In Britain the arrival of a Rolls Royce in a relatively depressed neighbourhood would arouse immediate suspicion, if not actual animosity – the feeling that someone was 'showing off' and deserved to be 'taken down peg or two'. If the car was left unattended, it might even be vandalized. It would certainly be regarded as a display of unnecessary opulence and the owner might well be looked on with a degree of contempt.

If the same thing occurred in the United States, I suspect there would be nothing but admiration for a person who had obviously 'made it' and was proudly enjoying the benefits of his or her success.

We really must try to rid ourselves of attitudes of guilt in regard to the making of money! This ridiculous British reserve is quite unnecessary. If we could learn to let go without reservation, recognize success and give credit to all those who, through their own efforts, achieve wealth ethically, we would all be the greater for it.

Success and the acquisition of wealth should never be regarded as suspect. Everyone has the chance to make something of his or her life and monetary achievement should be a matter for pride. Every successful person touches the lives of many others in all they do, often spreading the benefit of their own achievement so that the community in general is enriched.

Most really successful people understand the 'rules' of wealth – the reality of 'as you sow, so shall you reap'. Riches in life come about in many ways and we should always be prepared to put back into life in proportion to what we take out. Pay your dues and the rewards to you will be endless. . .

★

Getting back to the list . . .

It is now time to establish the more practical elements on our list. For example – earnings. In the light of everything you have established about yourself – your assets, acquired skills, abilities, and so on – decide what you feel you are worth. Don't under-sell yourself. Remember, the value you place upon yourself, will be the measure others will accept. Self-image, self-esteem, coupled with a good dash of ambition and self-belief! That is the recipe for your monetary decision.

Remember, it is not for you to question where these earnings are coming from – just accept that, with the right degree of desire and belief and the committed intention to do everything to stimulate movement and change in your life, things will happen! It will be for you to recognize the outcome and act on every thought and idea that comes at you, apparently 'out of the blue' – but, by now, you should have no doubts about what is actually at work.

And so, as before, write down your expectation of an earnings figure with a date by which it must be realized. Put the financial aspects down as a series of goals, if you wish. For example:

I will receive good ideas for making money
I will be able to repay all the money I owe on
credit cards
I will be enabled to pay off my overdraft with the bank
I will have a monthly income of £xxxx and I will
not owe a penny
etc

If you wish, put target dates against some of the items.

As before, in thinking about these things, it is important, when reading your list, to be able to enjoy the feeling of having extinguished your overdraft, paid off your credit cards etc. Experience the rosy glow of satisfaction these things will bring.

You should also add a few practical items to your list such as the car you want, the house you want and where it should ideally be. If you can obtain pictures of these requirements, as near to accurate as possible, do so, and paste them beside your statement so that everytime you read it you see it too!

Think about that house, wander through it, feel what it will be like to live there, what the view from the windows will be. Anything you can add to build as near a total picture of your desire and expectation will bring it closer to reality.

18. THE FINAL MOVE!

All that is required of you is to get on with your life, doing the things you know you have to do whilst following the dictates of your inner voice – the thing you might think of as 'inspiration' or 'intuition' or simple 'having ideas out of the blue'.

Don't hesitate to re-assess your targets from time to time and start the clock again. It may be that you have been over-ambitious and begin to lose your belief in the viability of the target you have set. Don't go battling blindly on, hoping that you can catch up. Regular under-achievement can have a very demotivational effect, so, as soon as the pattern is recognized, the immediate remedy will have to be applied – a bit of fine-tuning to re-establish a sensible target with all the correct motivational values.

By now you will probably appreciate that, if targets and goals are to serve the right purpose, they must be set with care, thought and precision, but kept just out of reach to ensure that you are always that little bit stretched.

A further refinement is, if you wish, to transfer each item on your list onto file cards or postcards, one item to each card. If you have pictures of any items on your list and they will fit onto the cards too, all the better.

Failing that, keep them with the cards so they are always available when you make your declarations.

You have now completed all your basic preparations. You have cleared away the rubbish and focused your attention on yourself in a way you have never done before so that you now have a very clear and uncluttered picture of the *you* you intend to be. Rather like the preparation of a garden, isn't it? – the seeds have been planted and will now have to be watered every day.

First thing each morning, immediately on rising, and last thing at night, just before getting into bed, find a quiet place where you can be on your own, and, standing before a mirror if possible, read aloud from your cards or list. You may find it difficult or possibly embarrassing to read your delarations out loud – and certainly, at first, you will feel a bit self-conscious doing it – but be sure you at least mouth the words, even if you feel it has to be in a whisper. The mind becomes so much more concentrated and focused when the words are actually spoken out loud.

This exercise can be repeated at any time during the day if you wish, but, whenever you do it, attempt to visualize what each card means to you. Build strong images. This is where the value of the actual pictures comes in. But create your own pictures and images as well until you feel the pleasure of whatever your desire might be. Enjoy the feel of the car, know what it is like to wander through the house, experience the pleasure of not owing money, and so on. The stronger the feelings are that you can generate, the easier the realization will become.

Whenever you are able to do so – any time, anywhere – go into your own very private inner silence for a few minutes – and listen. Empty your mind as completely as you are able and aim to be as receptive as possible. Always be aware that those little messages and instructions can come to you at any time. Always remember you are asking for help. It doesn't matter what or who you are asking – that is for you to decide. Because you are asking, when the answers come *act on them*.

Have you ever considered the nature of 'coincidence'? All those odd occasions when someone telephones you just as you are about to ring them. There are so many occasions in life when we are startled by these seemingly myusterious events – yet are they really so odd? If our minds have the ability to direct us towards change and success, it seems a very simple thing to pass small messages between like-minded people with a common intent. What about walking down the street and suddenly encountering someone you were just thinking about, often when you may not have met for a long time? We call it coincidence. But more than likely it was simply their proximity to you that caused you to think of them before you actually saw them. They were transmitting something that your listening self picked up.

Only the day before writing this I was in a large bookshop, standing in a queue approaching one of the tills. I thought I recognized the back view of the person standing in front of me and was on the point of tapping the man on the shoulder when I happened to see the very person I thought I was about to address in the queue at the other side of the shop! How one explains that, I don't really know – other than by saying it seemed to contain a confusion of messages.

Think about the events that you would call coincidence and see whether you can work out what actually happened.

We are walking around in possession of the most fabulous equipment that could be devised inside our heads, and yet we utilize about 5% of its potential. There are those who would have us believe that we are all merely part of one immense 'whole' and are linked through a collective intellect with the ability, if only we knew how to use it effectively, to draw on the entire accumulated knowledge of mankind. It has been thought to be a facility for which man has lost the use, and yet it has always been a most remarkable fact that scientists and inventors have been observed to arrive at parallel conclusions, or to invent the same thing in different parts of the world at precisely the same time – when they have had no contact whatsoever.

Be alert, listen, and be prepared to act on what you receive. Very often, immediately on waking, we get those little flashes of brilliance that are answers to questions and worries. They are the result of the subconscious night shift maintaining the service. When you have particular problems, use the facility available. Pose the question just before going to sleep and then *forget about it*. There is no point in keeping a dog and barking yourself! Last thing at night you are in no state to puzzle over problems and worries. All you achieve is to keep yourself awake, resulting in a restless night – because you are only using the simple functions of the surface facilities. Pose the question, outline the problem, let the night shift take over. Your immediate personal involvement has finished – empty your mind and go to sleep.

On waking the following morning, be very conscious of your thoughts. Be alert and *listen*. Don't expect miraculous messages for this is not the way things work. Sudden thoughts may flash across your consciousness; these are the things of which to take particular note. But do remember one thing; be prepared to act on the ideas you get and have faith in what you receive – remember the partially-sighted man and the fact that his survival depends on believing what he thinks he sees.

Doesn't it strike you as miraculous to realize what a wonderful mechanism you possess – and carry with you everywhere you go? The service that the sub-conscious offers is available to us all, but far too few people use it to any effect. So many people are over-sceptical and too willing to disregard the help they could receive, preferring to go their own way – as they could put it – in the belief that they are totally in control of their own lives. One thing you cannot do is to intellectualize with the subconscious. What I have called 'the service' is there to guide you. If you disagree with the ideas it presents, you are probably only procrastinating and that will lead to indecisive or even negative thought processes – and, by now, we know where those lead!

19. THE END OF THE JOURNEY – OR JUST THE BEGINNING?

Let's finally summarize our entire journey:
Before any change or modification takes place there is one thing you need to do – get used to the phrase *I AM RESPONSIBLE!* and consider all its implications.

1. *DESIRE*
   The desire for change. Nothing is possible without it.

2. *COMMITMENT*
   Any journey, no matter how long, starts with a single step.

3. *BELIEF*
   There must be total belief in the idea that change is possible – both change in self-image and self-esteem, and, through the complete process, change in both personal and surrounding circumstances.

4. **DECLARATIONS**
   Listing, ideally on separate cards, all the changes you intend to bring about, both in the development of personal attributes and achievement of material goals.

5. **VISUALIZATION**
   The imagery of belief. Developing strong mental pictures of all you desire – and looking at actual pictures to reinforce that desire so as to enable you to really 'feel' the object or situation.

6. **KNOW YOUR SUBCONSCIOUS**
   Get on intimate terms with it. Develop the habit of quiet moments in a quiet place. Listen – believe – act.

7. **ASK QUESTIONS**
   Make 'the service' operate for you in a definite way.

8. **ACCEPT ANSWERS**
   Take notice. Listen. . .

9. **ACTION!**
   Act on the ideas you receive. Act on hunches and intuitive thoughts.
   Be hold! Be positive! Remember – this is the new you!

These are the simple techniques that can bring about the very thing we have been working towards –

the shaping of the new you, the person, perhaps, that you have always wanted to be.

The entire aim of this book has been to make you think. To think about the YOU that was, that is, and that will be. To create self-awareness and build a new self-image. To get you to walk tall, acquire a sense of your own value and total uniqueness and, above all, to believe in your ability to alter circumstances. Be aware of the fact that **there has never before, in the history of mankind, been a person just like you, and never will there be again a person just like you.**

I see a danger in suggesting too much to you as I could be instrumental in causing you to take the line of least resistance by relying too much on my suggestions – on the other hand, anything I suggest might prove to be your salvation! What a dilemma, and what a responsibility!

I know that I have put forward ideas that some will find distinctly fanciful. All I would say is examine everything that comes your way. Don't be too dismissive about *anything*. There are other ideas I would like to put to you but, if you have found this book interesting and helpful, I feel sure that you will come across many illuminating things for yourself through your increased awareness. You will find other ideas and techniques for self-development – and it is far better that you evaluate these for yourself. All I have done is present you with a simple, basic structure upon which to build . . .

My great hope is that, in offering you your starting point, I may have been able to show you that the habit of success is an achievable goal in itself.

I want to conclude by wishing you the greatest possible success in all you undertake. If this book is truly beneficial to you I would be delighted to hear from you – who knows, we might have the basis for a follow-up book of success stories!

Remember again what Henry Ford said – 'If you believe you can do a thing, or if you believe you cannot – *you are right*.' I hope that in this journey we have taken together I have demonstrated there is never any point in believing that you can't. All that remains to be said is simply –

. . . BELIEVE YOU CAN!

20. P. S.

Many people have come across 'Desiderata' – a document dated 1692 that was found in Old Saint Paul's Church, Baltimore, USA. It is so full of profound and straight-forward wisdom, I include it here, for it has quite a lot to do with the journey we have taken together.

DESIDERATA

Go placidly amid the noise and haste and remember what peace there may be in silence. As far as possible without surrender be on good terms with all persons. Speak your truth quietly and clearly; and listen to others, even the dull and ignorant; they too have their story.

Avoid loud and aggressive persons, they are vexations to the spirit. If you compare yourself with others, you may become vain and bitter; for always there will be greater and lesser persons than yourself. Enjoy your achievements as well as your plans.

Keep interested in your own career, however humble; it is a real possession in the changing fortunes of time. Exercise caution in your business affairs; for the world is full of trickery. But let this not blind you to what virtue there is; many persons strive for high ideals; and everywhere life is full of heroism.

Be yourself. Especially, do not feign affection. Neither be cynical about love: for in the face of all aridity and disenchantment it is perennial as the grass.

Take kindly the counsel of the years, gracefully surrendering the things of youth. Nurture strength of spirit to shield you in sudden misfortune. But do not distress yourself with imaginings. Many fears are born of fatigue and loneliness. Beyond a wholesome discipline, be gentle with yourself.

You are a child of the universe, no less than the trees and the stars; you have a right to be here. And whether or not it is clear to you, no doubt the universe is unfolding as it should.

Therefore be at peace with God, whatever you conceive Him to be, and whatever your labors and aspirations, in the noisy confusion of life keep peace with your soul.

With all its sham, drudgery and broken dreams, it is still a beautiful world. Be careful. Strive to be happy.

ORDER FORM (BYC)

To: Concept
P.O. Box 614
Polegate
East Sussex
BN26 5SS, 0323 485434

There are many companies and other organizations that will recognize the benefit that this book could be to their particular operation. We offer substantial discounts on bulk orders. Please contact us on the above telephone number or at the address given for further details.

ALLEN CARMICHAEL BOOKS

Please send me .... copies of 'BELIEVE YOU CAN!' at £6.99 per copy plus P&P (see note below)

Please send me .... copies of 'NETWORK & MULTI-LEVEL MARKETING' at £4.99 per copy plus P&P (see note below)

Please send me .... copies of 'THE NETWORK MARKETING SELF-STARTER' at £6.95 per copy plus P&P (see note below)

Name: ....

Address: ....

Post Code .... Telephone ....

Note P&P charges: 1 book – .49p   2 books – .84p
3 books – £1.35

It would be helpful to know where you purchased this book:

....

REGISTRATION FORM (BYC)

To: Concept
P.O. Box 614
Polegate,
East Sussex
BN26 5SS

*Please add my name to your mailing list and send me news
and information about future CONCEPT publications.*

Title: Mr Mrs Miss _____

Forenames: _____

Surname: _____

Address: _____

_____

_____ Postcode: _____

Telephone number: _____